Lloyd Aéreo Boliviano

In the Shadow of the Condor

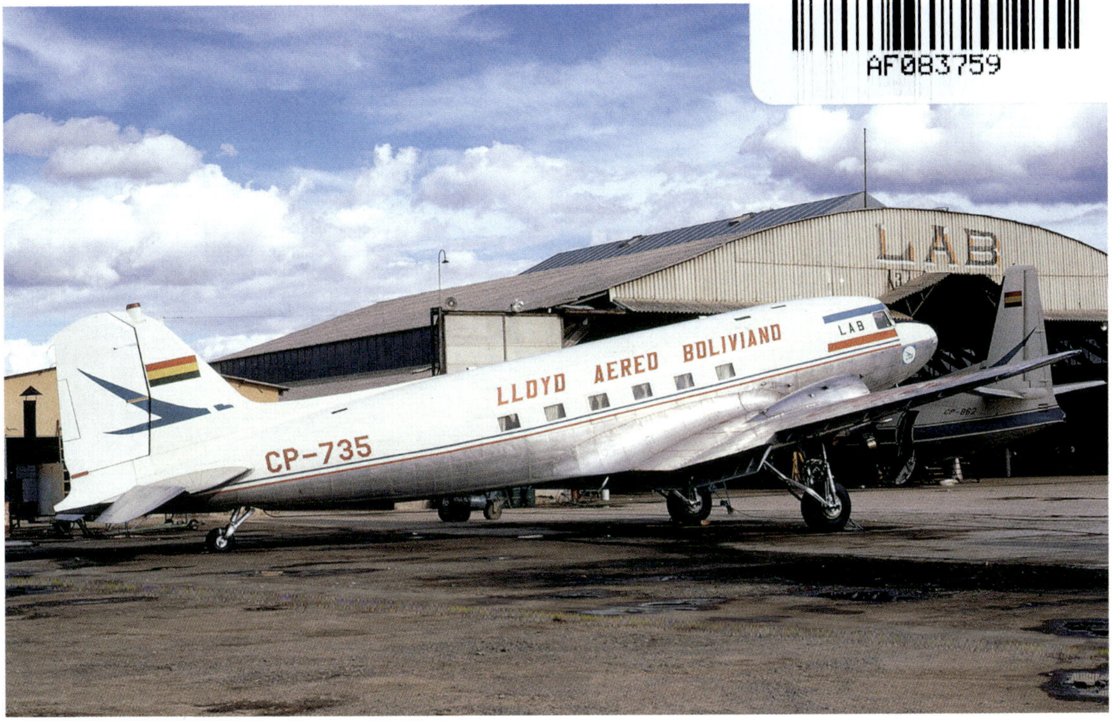

BARRY LLOYD

KEY Books

AIRLINES SERIES, VOLUME 8

Front cover image: A typical Andean scene with Boeing 727-100 series CP-1223, the aircraft with the highest number of cycles of all Boeing 727s. (Michael Prophet)

Contents page image: The cargo door on this LAB Boeing 707-323C is clearly visible as it makes its final approach to Miami. (Bob O'Brien Collection)

Published by Key Books
An imprint of Key Publishing Ltd
PO Box 100
Stamford
Lincs PE19 1XQ

www.keypublishing.com

The right of Barry Lloyd to be identified as the author of this book has been asserted in accordance with the Copyright, Designs and Patents Act 1988 Sections 77 and 78.

Copyright © Barry Lloyd, 2022

ISBN 978 1 80282 241 0

All rights reserved. Reproduction in whole or in part in any form whatsoever or by any means is strictly prohibited without the prior permission of the Publisher.

Typeset by SJmagic DESIGN SERVICES, India.

Contents

Introduction 4

Chapter 1 1925–45: Early days and the lead-up to war with Paraguay 8

Chapter 2 1945–60: Recovery from the war and sustained growth 21

Chapter 3 1960–70: Difficult times 34

Chapter 4 1970–90: Steady growth 42

Chapter 5 1990–2007 66

Addendum 81

LAB fleet list 83

Introduction

Ask the average person in the street about their knowledge of Bolivia and they will probably conjure up thoughts of ladies in bowler hats and perhaps the sound of pan pipes. While these images can still be found in Bolivia, they represent just a very small part of a country that is little-known outside Latin America. Bolivia, officially the Plurinational State of Bolivia, is a large, landlocked country, twice the size of France, or 1.6 times the size of Texas. The country is characterised by the High Andes to the west, known as the Altiplano (Spanish for 'high plains'). The Altiplano originates northwest of Lake Titicaca in southern Peru and extends about 600 miles (966km) southeast towards the southwestern corner of Bolivia. On the eastern side of the Altiplano exists a gentle gradient that extends southwards across Bolivia. The eastern side of the country, which lies behind the shadow of the Andes, is known as the llanos or plains, but more generally as the Oriente (east), which comprises more than 60 per cent of Bolivia's total land mass. It covers an approximate area of 250,000 square miles (600,000km^2) and extends from the foothills of the Andes to the River Paraguay. It is also where much of the food in Bolivia is grown and exported from. Being less than 20 degrees south of the equator, the region has a humid, tropical climate, with a typical daily temperature of 25°C (77°F). The land is largely flat, with many plateaus fed by numerous rivers. The wind, when driven through the Amazon rainforest, can bring about significant rainfall.

The major cities in the Altiplano are the judicial and constitutional capital Sucre, which sits at a height of 9,220ft (2,810m) above sea level, while La Paz, which is the seat of the government, as well as the legislative and executive capital, sits at 11,942ft (3,640m) above sea level and is generally regarded as the world's highest capital city. As if this were not enough, the airport serving La Paz lies at 13,323ft (4,061m) on a plain 8 miles (13km) west of La Paz, making it the highest international airport in the world and justifying its title of El Alto (The High One). Regarded as the fourth largest city, La Paz and El Alto are classified as separate regions, followed by Santa Cruz. Cochabamba lies at 8,932ft (2,722m) above sea level and was the headquarters of Lloyd Aéreo Boliviano (LAB). The fact that, despite its altitude, it is known as 'The City of Eternal Spring', thanks to its temperate climate, may have played a part in the decision to make this LAB's headquarters. It is the unique topography of Bolivia that sets it apart from its neighbours, in every sense.

There are three main regions in Bolivia: the Andean region, which, as the name suggests, is part of the Andes mountain range; the Sub-Andean region in the centre and south of the country; and the llanos (plains) region, in the northeast of the country. With such diverse topography, it stands to reason that there are great variations in the climate throughout the country. The eastern llanos are tropical – most months are hot and humid, and the land is fed by rivers that are large tributaries of the Amazon, and sometimes prone to flooding. More than 70 per cent of all the cattle in Bolivia are raised on this land. This is quite a remote region where, even today, there is less than 1,243 miles (2,000km) of paved road. Further west, ambient temperatures are cooler, reaching out towards the Andes, where snow falls on the highest parts of the region.

Rain is frequent in all the regions, with strong winds common in the llanos region. The atmospheric pressure (a critical factor in determining aircraft altitude) varies enormously between the Andes, which run from Colombia in the north to Chile in the south and account for about 28 per cent of Bolivia's total land area, all of which sits at 9,800ft (3,000m) above sea level. The region actually lies between two mountain ranges – the western range and the central range – and within that are some of the highest mountains in the Americas. This is the Altiplano. The Altiplano has numerous lakes and rivers that do not run to the sea because they are enclosed by the Andean mountains. The El Niño phenomenon exists not far from the Pacific coast in this area and can have a significant impact on the weather pattern.

The Sub-Andes is an intermediate range of mountains that lies in the centre and south of the country, between the Altiplano and the llanos. It is here that aircraft were forced to operate in the earlier years of LAB's operations, accounting for many of the accidents the airline suffered. The Sub-Andes makes up about 13 per cent of Bolivian territory. The high ground gradually gives way to the valleys and the Yungas region. The land is mainly agricultural, and the climate is temperate, but snow falls on the mountains above 6,600ft (2,000m) and the region is humid and subject to a lot of rain.

On the Altiplano, there are only two seasons; the summers can be warm and wet, except in the extremely high areas such as La Paz and Potosí, and the winters are dry and cold. The Andes are up to 500 miles (800km) wide in places and split into two ranges, known as the Eastern and Western Cordillera. On the eastern edge are deep valleys. Lake Titicaca, the world's highest lake, covering almost the same area as Puerto Rico and totally navigable, lies to the northwest of the country and borders Peru. It is situated at an elevation of 12,500ft (3,810m), and plays a very important part in maintaining the climatic condition of the nearby land, making it eminently suitable for the growing of cereal crops. Agriculture forms a large part of the Bolivian economy, but it is also known for its large tin deposits – though little is left nowadays – together with mineral and gas resources. Bolivia extends from north to south between 10° and 23° south of the equator, a distance of 932 miles (1,500km) and from the western edge of the Andes to Brazil, a distance of 808 miles (1,300km). The highest mountain in Bolivia, which is in fact an extinct volcano, is the Nevado Sajama, standing at 21,463ft (6,542m), but there are five other peaks that rise above 20,000ft (6,100m). Bolivia shares borders with Argentina, Brazil, Chile, Paraguay and Peru.

In comparison to its neighbours, Argentina, Brazil and Chile, Bolivia has a larger wealth disparity amongst its citizens, though the discovery of natural gas within the last 15 years has started to change this. The population consists of about 85 per cent Indigenous people, who statistically have had lower than average literacy levels. This has meant that a small elite group have generally led the country. Usually, people in this group have had military backgrounds or were part of prominent family hierarchies. This, to some degree, accounts for the constant changes in governments. This has played a factor in the beginnings, the development and the daily operation of LAB, and it is worth examining the country's background in order to fully understand the challenges the airline has faced since its inception.

Since its independence from Spain in 1825, Bolivia's constant political upheavals have upset the country's stability, and this has had a significant effect on its economy and thus the exchange rate of the national currency. Like most Latin American countries, Bolivia's currency is tied to the dollar, thus the constant exchange-rate fluctuations, normally to the disadvantage of the Bolivian economy, have made life difficult for everyone. If this were not enough, constant political changes have dogged the country since its independence from Spain. In more recent times, a military junta overthrew President Victor Paz Estenssoro in 1964, as he was beginning his third term in office. A series of weak governments followed until the military installed General Hugo Banzer as president in 1971. The previous president, Juan José Torres (October 1970–August 1971) was popular with the people but not with the military. He was deposed and exiled to Argentina, where he was murdered. His body was found under a bridge 63 miles (100km) from Buenos Aires in June 1976.

The Central Intelligence Agency (CIA) of the US, ever watchful of the changing events in Latin America for fear of communism taking a strong hold on politics, financed and trained Banzer's military dictatorship. The Bolivian Armed Forces had been trained by the US and supported by the CIA, and it was as a result of this activity that Che Guevara was killed on 9 October 1967, in the southern province of Vallegrande.

Elections in 1979 were inconclusive, and there were allegations of fraud. In 1980, the repressive General Luis García Meza seized power, but it was rumoured in local circles that his government was heavily involved in drug trafficking and thus had links to criminal groups, a fact that soon became public knowledge. There was an international outcry, sufficient enough to force Meza's resignation in 1981. A further election followed, but this was inconclusive. His successor was the equally repressive General Celso Torrelio Villa. His dictatorship lasted for only a year. The Bolivian military, by now severely blemished by its connections to corruption at every level, returned to barracks and has never been in power since. The unrest engendered by the dictatorship meant that the military was asked to reconvene the Congress, which had been in power only in 1980, in order to choose a new chief executive. In October 1982, Hernán Siles was returned to the presidency at the age of 68, following his earlier presidency between 1956 and 1960.

From this, it can be seen that an unstable political situation did nothing to help Bolivia's already weak economy and, by extension, LAB. At one point in 1985, Bolivia was suffering from a staggering inflation rate of 11,750 per cent, a figure unimaginable to most. To put this into a Bolivian perspective, in 1982, 64 Bolivian pesos (which was then the standard currency) was the equivalent to one US dollar. By 1983, it was 230 pesos, and, by 1984, it had risen to 2,314. During 1985, one million pesos were needed to buy a single US dollar; this was the black-market rate. As a result, the president declared a free exchange rate for the peso, so that in August 1985, it devalued by 95 per cent. Exchange controls were lifted, and a fixed exchange rate was set twice weekly, based on supply and demand. However, the value of the peso continued to fall, and, in January 1986, the government was setting a daily exchange rate in order to bolster the economy. During this time, the peso reached a low point of 2.2 million pesos per one dollar, later stabilising to 1.85 million. In late 1986, a monetary reform law was passed, which discontinued the peso. The Bolivian currency became the boliviano, with one million old pesos equivalent to one boliviano. The boliviano was initially introduced on a one-for-one basis against the dollar.

With such a background, it is not difficult to understand how LAB struggled with inflation and the relative value of its country's currency against the dollar. There was a continuous battle to maintain the equilibrium by all businesses simply to pay salaries, taxes, pension schemes, etc. Furthermore, in aviation, many major costs have to be paid for in dollars, so the purchase of aircraft, foreign training, spare parts and fuel when outside of the country has to be set against a constantly devaluing local currency. Since major portions of LAB's routes were domestic and the majority of tickets were paid for in local currency, there was the constant need to balance the books against currency fluctuations. LAB's focus had always been on opening and maintaining domestic routes, encouraged by the government – no surprise, given the size of the country and the poor overland infrastructure. All efforts were focused on connecting the country, and little attention was paid to developing international routes, especially given the constant disagreements with Bolivia's neighbours.

Compared to the more well-known tourist destinations in South America, Bolivia sees little in the way of foreign tourism. Visitor figures have remained steady in recent years – prior to the COVID-19 pandemic, it was just below one million visitors per year. Its neighbour Peru attracts about 4 million visitors, but even when compared with the lesser-visited countries of Uruguay (2 million) and Colombia (4.5 million), the figure is low. This means the opportunity for LAB to earn hard-currency revenue from visitor air fares has always been very limited.

Introduction

Since its independence from Spain, Bolivia has experienced more than 190 coups d'état and revolutions – more than any other country. On 3 October 1970, it actually had five presidents installed during the course of a single day. It has also been involved in a number of wars, one of which was with Chile in the 1880s and resulted in Bolivia losing direct access to the sea. The defeat meant that 249 miles (400km) of coastline, which was formerly Bolivian, passed to Chile. Later, in 1904, a ruling by the International Court of Justice declared that Chile had not kept diplomatic promises and obligations under international law to allow sea access. Chile agreed to compensate Bolivia for its loss of land and allowed it access to Chilean ports. The second war was with Brazil over the Acre region, an area five times the size of Belgium and rich in rubber and gold deposits. This took place in two phases between 1899 and 1903. Acre won the battle, which was followed by the Treaty of Petrópolis, ceding the territory to Brazil. The third, and arguably the most damaging, was the Gran Chaco War, which is covered later in this book.

Perhaps the biggest blow to the Bolivian economy was the collapse of tin prices in the 1980s. This was one of the few, but major, sources of income in Bolivia and earned the country much-needed foreign income. Following this, the government implemented a stabilisation programme, with the intention of having greater control over the economy and, thus, stabilising prices and promoting growth. A major reform of the customs service was also introduced, with the intention of deterring smuggling — an activity which does much to undermine the economies of the Andean nations. Foreign investment, particularly in the telecommunications and oil industries, was also encouraged. In more recent times, prosperity has improved in Bolivia, thanks to the discovery of natural gas. It has what is believed to be the second largest reserves of natural gas in South America, much of which is exported to Brazil.

It is against this background then, that LAB led its daily life. Initially, it had to contend with linking the llanos to the mid-Andes and later to the Altiplano. The lack of weather forecasting made flying all the more difficult and dangerous, and it is fair to say that few airlines have had to face such challenges from the very beginning. Add in the numerous political upheavals and it could be said that it is surprising that LAB lasted as long as it did. This book will explain the numerous challenges the airline faced, together with the political and financial chicanery that led to its eventual demise.

Chapter 1
1925–45:
Early days and the lead-up to war with Paraguay

From the beginning of the 20th century, much like other countries in the region, there was a significant German community in Bolivia. They had quickly identified the difficulties involved with the provision of surface transport throughout the country and had recognised the potential of air travel to overcome this. Guillermo Kyllmann, the manager of a German importing company, was one of the driving forces behind the project, assisted by Hans Grether, a civil engineer, who had been tasked with building a railway from Cochabamba to Santa Cruz. Grether's numerous surveys had revealed the problems of such a project: apart from the rugged terrain, there were difficulties with the heat and humidity and also the dense vegetation that existed on the planned route. These potential difficulties were sufficient to convince him that air travel would be a better solution. Thus, Grether joined Kyllmann in lobbying the government, industry and commerce, together with the remainder of the population, to make all of them aware of how air travel could overcome the problems of surface transport.

The rugged nature of Bolivia, with its mountains, valleys and plains, up to a third of which could be flooded during the rainy season, meant the building of roads and railways would also be extremely expensive and simply impossible in some cases, as Grether had discovered. Two-thirds of Bolivia's population inhabited the mountainous areas, with the remainder living in the eastern plains and, therefore, there was a complete imbalance in traffic. Any development of surface transport was thus concentrated in the more populous mountain areas of the west. So acute was this situation that, until 1960, almost 40 per cent of Bolivia had no land connection to other areas, and the only routes were by steamer ferries across Lake Titicaca or by air. There was an urgent need to link the highlands with the valleys and the plains. A United Nations mission, which visited the country in 1950, declared that the importance of air travel in Bolivia could not be over-estimated, citing the lack of surface routes over almost three-quarters of the nation's territory.

Headed by Hans Grether, the German consortium persuaded the people of their homeland to donate an aircraft to the Bolivian government, rather than the usual statue or plaque, to celebrate the centenary of Bolivia's independence from Spain. In July 1925, a Junkers F 13 arrived – a gift from the people of Germany. It had been transported by train from Buenos Aires and was therefore unassembled. The F 13 was a small low-winged aircraft with a solid fuselage made of metal alloys. It had a single six-cylinder BMW IV engine and was designed to carry four passengers. Junkers sent a representative to oversee the assembly and flight test the aircraft. It was named *El Oriente*, the name given to the eastern region of Bolivia. Junkers also took a number of shares in the new company; thus, LAB was established. Founded in 1925, LAB was the second carrier to be established in South America, after SCADTA, a Colombian airline also founded with German interests, in 1919. The F 13 made its first test flight on 27 July 1925. Just four and a half years later, LAB was operating the fourth largest

Mamore, together with another unidentified F 13, sits on a river in northern Bolivia. (Folab)

network in Latin America, behind Mexico, Argentina and Peru. It was comparable with that of Condor Syndikat, based in Brazil.

A few days later, the aircraft was flown from Cochabamba to Sucre, which at that time had been declared the capital of Bolivia. It was a high-profile display, coinciding with the centenary of Bolivia's independence. On 2 August 1925, two passengers paid to fly over Cochabamba for 20 minutes. One month later, on 15 September, the formal documents were issued authorising shares in the new airline. The company would operate under a board of directors based in La Paz, but the administration office would work out of Cochabamba. This marked the beginning of the LAB story, and in recognition of his enthusiasm for setting up the airline and promoting Bolivian aviation, Guillermo Kyllman was elected as president of the airline.

With the initial flight-proving complete, new routes were approved and proper procedures began to take shape. The aircraft was insured, following which it was allowed to carry mail for no charge (normally, a postal service pays a premium for carrying mail by air, so this was most unusual) and LAB also agreed to carry senior functionaries of the government for a 30 per cent discount. The first regular service between Cochabamba and Santa Cruz took place on 24 December 1925. The flight lasted about 2 hours 20 minutes, covering the 200 miles (320km) between the cities. This compared very favourably with the land-based alternatives which, depending on weather and other factors, could take between

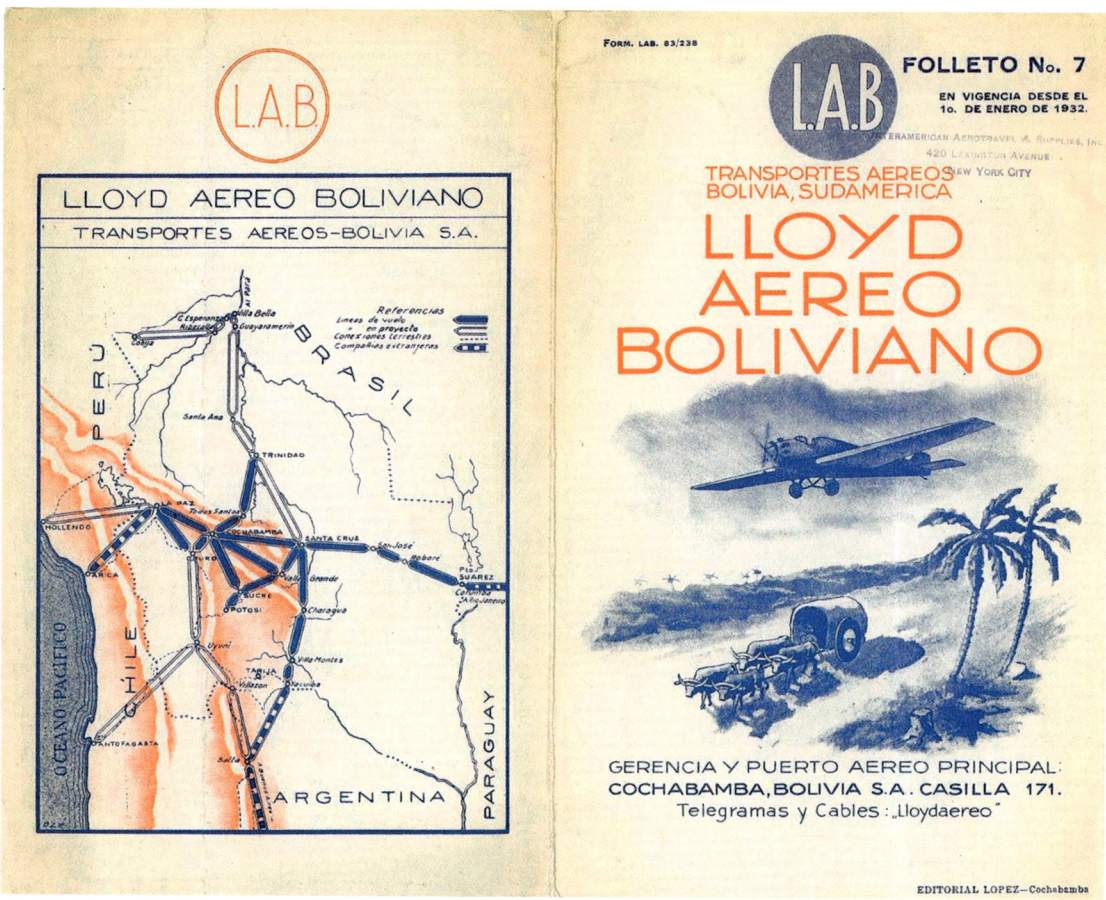

A copy of the 1932 LAB timetable, showing the route network. On the left panel, top right-hand side, from top to bottom, the legend is as follows: current routes, projected routes, overland connections, foreign airlines. (Bjorn Larsson/timetableimages.com)

four days and two weeks. With this result, enthusiasm for the airline project grew rapidly, and as such, a second aircraft arrived on 15 September 1926.

At this time, the aircraft were not fitted with radios, and Bolivia did not have a formal registration system for its aircraft, so they were simply named after regions within the country. Annex 7 of the Convention on International Civil Aviation describes the details of the nationality of registration marks. This, in turn, is taken from the callsign prefix allocated by the International Telecommunications Union. In respect of this, a meeting took place at the International Radiotelegraph Convention in Washington in 1927, at which the list of registration markings was revised and adopted from 1928; these are now the basis of current aircraft registrations throughout the world. Because the aircraft in LAB service were not equipped with radios, they continued to name any new aircraft that arrived after a region of the country, with the name being applied to the side of the aircraft in large letters. Navigation was carried out by the pilots using nearby towns and the few roads as landmarks. The registration allocated to Bolivia was originally C-B and was used from 1919 to 1929. The prefix CB- followed by numbers was introduced from 1929 and used until 1954. In 1954, CP- was introduced. Aircraft still in operation that originally had the CB- registration were allocated new numbers with the CP- prefix.

On 6 November 1926, LAB experienced its first accident. On a flight between Cochabamba and Santa Cruz, the aircraft encountered bad weather and had to be force-landed. The three passengers and two crew survived uninjured, but the aircraft, *El Oriente*, LAB's first to be operated, was a write-off. A replacement aircraft was ordered, and it finally arrived in Bolivia in early 1927. It was named *Oriente II*. A new route to Trinidad, the principal town in the rich pasturelands of the lowland Beni region, known as the Oriente, was opened on 28 October 1926. A further three aircraft were delivered during 1928. With these aircraft incorporated into the fleet, a new service to the Mamoré region in the centre of the country was introduced. After a couple of losses, the fleet in 1928 numbered six; *Oriente II, Charcas, Mamoré, Illimani, Chaco* and *Beni III*. Significantly, two of the aircraft were fitted with floats, enabling them to operate on the large rivers, tributaries of the Amazon, found in the north of the country.

With traffic continually increasing, LAB set up an aviation school for the training of pilots and engineers. The first pilot to graduate from this school was Jorge Wilstermann Camacho, after whom the airport at Cochabamba is now named. LAB continued to expand the route network and, in July 1930, opened a route to Corumbá, a Brazilian town close to the northeastern border with Bolivia. This became LAB's first international flight. From here, there was a flight operated by the German-owned Brazilian airline, Condor Syndikat, which, via several stops en route, was able to offer flights to Rio de Janeiro, and from there to the rest of South America and beyond.

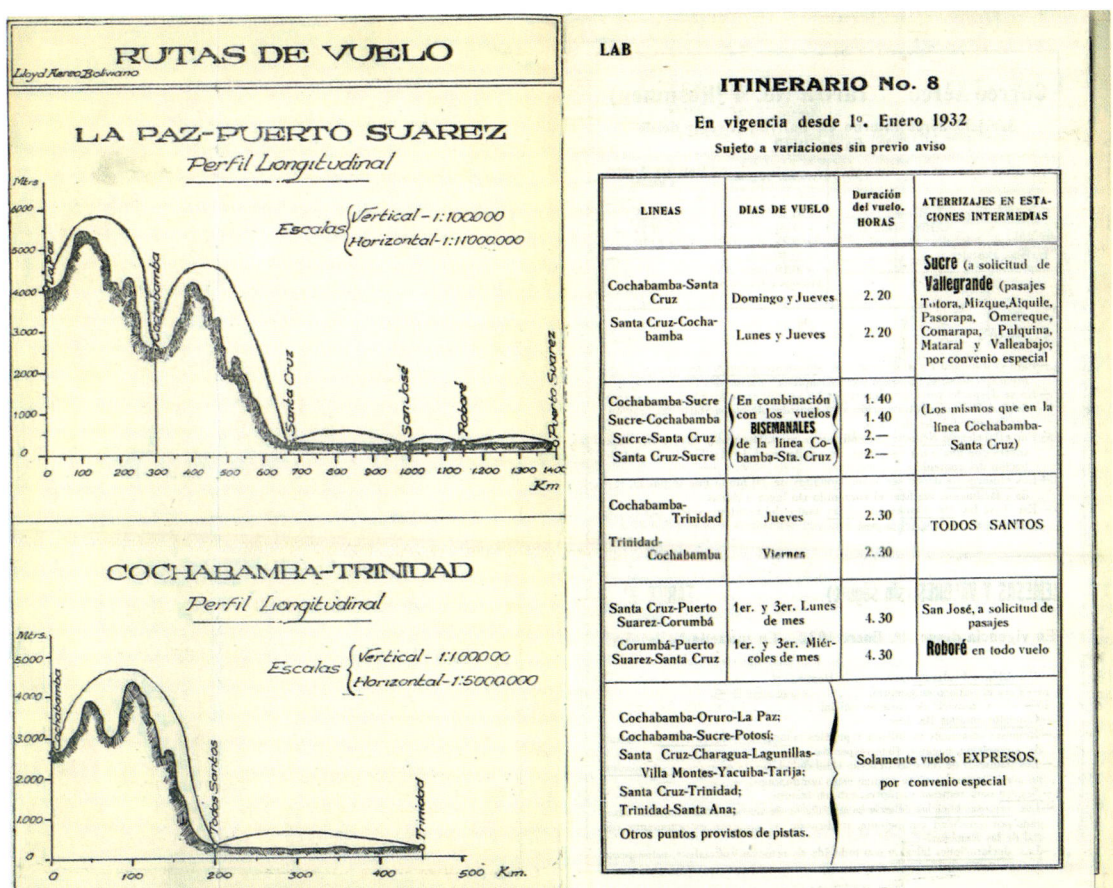

Another copy of a 1932 timetable, showing in graphic form the topography of Bolivia. Altitude is on the left and distance is on the right (both in metres). (Bjorn Larsson/timetableimages.com)

In 1925, an F 13 publicity flight took place over the city of Cochabamba in the centre of the country. Several further flights came after, followed by subsequent flights to other cities, such as Sucre, Potosí and Santa Cruz. The first scheduled departure to Sucre took place on 5 August 1925. This was the first official point-to-point flight for fare-paying customers, as previous trips had been more along the lines of 'pleasure flights'. The flight took an hour and a half. A similar journey by road would have taken ten hours in those days. At that time, LAB was based in Cochabamba, but as the network grew, more flights began to operate from Santa Cruz. On 16 August 1925, President Bautista Saavedra, together with the Archbishop of Santa Cruz, officially handed over the aircraft to what would become Lloyd Aéreo Boliviano. It is believed that the name Lloyd was incorporated to lend additional credibility to the company, as the name was associated with the famous London-based underwriters, renowned for its image of safety and security. In 1926, the government began to invest in the internal infrastructure of the country, allowing LAB to operate to the capitals of three Bolivian states by 1928. By 1930, LAB had the fourth largest route network in South America and was able to use 34 landing strips, many of which the army had helped to develop. In addition, further runways were under construction, along with three emergency runways. In September 1931, the government delegated the construction of runways to LAB itself.

The airline continued to grow; a Junkers W 34 arrived in March 1929. This was named *Vanguardia* and was followed a year later by a second aircraft, *Tunari*. The advantage of the W 34 was in its more powerful engines and its ability to carry six passengers in comparison with the four seats offered by the F 13. However, just as the airline was beginning to see the beginnings of stability and economic development, the clouds of war began to gather.

From the beginning, LAB's task was to connect the Altiplano with the llanos. This was never going to be easy, given the height of the Andes in this area and the relative power of the aircraft involved at the time, together with a total lack of navigational aids and only landing strips to use as airports. It should be noted that none of the routes served La Paz at this time. The rapidly changing weather conditions in the mountains were an added factor. The alternative, since there were no railways, was to traverse the Andes by road, and while bus services did exist, the roads over the mountains were little more than passes and fatal accidents were frequent. Bolivia is the home of the infamous El Camino de la Muerte (Death Road) which runs between La Paz and the central region of Los Yungas.

Aviation was very much in its infancy at this point, with airfields being little more than a runway fashioned from a strip of flat land. It was not until the late 1930s that the first airports, or passenger stations as they were rather quaintly named locally, were constructed. The first was El Alto in La Paz. This was built in 1937, and then followed by El Trompillo (Santa Cruz) and Cochabamba in 1939. In other towns, such as Potosí and Tarija, the available facilities had been provided by the local municipalities.

Perhaps surprisingly, it was not until 1965 that the government set up a formal body, the Administration of Airports and Auxiliary Services to Air Navigation (AASANA), to oversee the construction and operation of airfields in Bolivia.

The Gran Chaco War

The Gran Chaco is a very large area of open land, in the in Rio de la Plata (River Plate) basin. The territory is currently divided between eastern Bolivia, western Paraguay, northern Argentina and the eastern portion of the Brazilian states of Mato Grosso and Mato Grosso do Sul. At 303,782 square miles (786,791km^2), it is approximately the same size as Turkey. The war is little-known beyond the borders of Bolivia and Paraguay. It was fought between the two countries over a territory to which both laid claim. The war is generally considered to have begun over oil deposits that had

The Curtiss-Wright CW-14, as used in the Gran Chaco War (LAB)

been found in a largely undeveloped region in the border areas. In 1929, a series of border incidents led to the breaking off of diplomatic relations and then war. The Bolivians believed that their army, which had been trained by the Germans and was well-equipped, would overwhelm the Paraguayans but, in fact, Paraguay won all the major battles. Almost 65,000 Bolivians lost their lives as a result of the conflict.

The Treaty of Lima, signed on 3 June 1929, had decreed that Bolivia no longer held access to the sea, which Bolivia feared would have a significant effect on its economy, particularly with regard to tin exports. A conflict between two oil companies that were competing for drilling rights in the region served to exacerbate the situation. Royal Dutch Shell was backing Paraguay, while Standard Oil of the US (the forerunner of Esso, later Exxon), was supporting Bolivia. In addition, both Paraguay and Bolivia were landlocked, but the Paraguay River runs through the region and offers access to the Atlantic, and this was of particular interest to Bolivia, as it had lost its access to the Pacific to Chile in the War of the Pacific. Equally, Paraguay had lost almost half of its territory to both Brazil and Argentina in the War of the Triple Alliance fought between 1864 and 1870.

The Chaco War lasted from 1932 to 1935 and was particularly notable because it became the first large-scale air war to take place in South America. In fact, as an aerial war, it probably had a greater resemblance to World War One in Europe but was nevertheless fought with considerable determination. The Bolivians used possibly as many as 20 CW-14R Ospreys, a single-engined biplane built by Curtiss-Wright in the US in the early 1930s. The aircraft arrived in batches of 12, six and three, but the

CB-26 was a Lockheed Lodestar that crashed after being hit by government anti-aircraft fire while on a supporting flight for rebels during a civil war. (Folab)

last aircraft in the batch was seized by Chilean customs following an embargo imposed by the League of Nations, the forerunner of the United Nations. There was an order for a further six aircraft, but this was cancelled in the light of the Chilean seizure. All but the first two aircraft were issued with incidental serial numbers, the first two having been written off before the serials were applied. The aircraft were formed into a unit reflecting the aircraft's name: Osprey Escuadrilla. The first time it saw service was on 2 January 1933, when the Bolivians attacked a Paraguayan troop concentration in the town of Nanawa. Just a few weeks later, the first aircraft involved in the air battle was shot down. A strike force of Ospreys was then assembled and launched from their base at Muñoz to attack Puerto Casado, but the Argentinians raised a diplomatic objection, which meant that Bolivia could not make any further attacks along the Paraguay River.

The Paraguayans, for their part, had the French-built Potez 25, a single-engined biplane, not unlike the Osprey but built a little earlier, in the mid-1920s. Six of these were the A 2 model, while the remaining eight were the TOE variant. The type had sold widely around the world. At the time, Argentina officially stayed neutral throughout the conflict, though it is known it was supplying Paraguay with war materiel. When the armistice took place in June 1935, only three Bolivian aircraft remained, the rest having been either shot down or crashed. A request was sent to the US for spare parts for two of the remaining aircraft, but it was refused. The third remained with the Fuerza Aérea Boliviana (FAB, Bolivian Air Force) until 1954.

Bolivia also used devious means to try to import several Curtiss T-32 Condor II twin-engined bombers, disguised as transport aircraft, ostensibly for use by LAB, but they were stopped in Peru while en route. This was a large biplane, capable of being used in both the transport and bomber roles. Following the seizure of the Condors, the Bolivian government had to sequester all of LAB's aircraft and staff, so they could be converted for military use, taking troops and war materiel to the front line to assist with the war effort. In December 1932, three Junkers 52/3ms arrived. These had been bought with a loan offered by the Bolivian business tycoon Simón Patiño and were registered CB-17, 18 and 21. At that time, Bolivia was one of the largest producers of tin in the world, and Patiño was one of the wealthiest people in the world, having bult his fortune from ownership of the tin mining industry. He was a staunch supporter of Bolivia and LAB. Nicknamed the Andean Rockefeller, he suffered from bad health, and in 1924, he sustained a heart attack and was advised not to return to Bolivia. He moved abroad permanently and died in Buenos Aires in 1947.

Two further aircraft were delivered and registered as CB-22 and CB-32. The fact that the Ju 52s could carry a 3-tonne payload made them ideal for transporting supplies to Bolivian troops. It is believed that during the Chaco War, the Ju 52s alone flew more than 4,400 tonnes of cargo in support of Bolivia's fight for the Gran Chaco. However, it was to no avail, as the disputed territory was eventually awarded to Paraguay, and the Junkers were absorbed into LAB's civil fleet. LAB also operated a single Ford Trimotor, originally unregistered but named *Cruz del Sur (Southern Cross)*. This was written off near the town of Villamontes in the Gran Chaco region on 26 October 1932, while conveying supplies to the Bolivian Army.

During the war, LAB's aircraft had been involved in supporting troops, with all operations paid for by the government. Now there was little traffic, several of the aircraft had crashed and the fleet was decimated. Later, two single-engined Junkers W 33s were added to the fleet. These differed from the W 34s only in engine size, and soon afterwards a further two Ju 52/3ms joined the airline. With these additions to the fleet, by 1936 LAB was operating 11 aircraft, including three F 13s and a Sikorsky S-38B – a twin-engined biplane capable of carrying between eight and ten passengers. A similar aircraft had been used by Pan American and Charles Lindbergh to inaugurate an air mail service between the US and the Panama Canal. It was an unusual looking aircraft, which first flew in May 1928. Its big advantage was that it was an amphibian, and since useful landing strips were still rudimentary and often far-flung, and as there are a number of large rivers in Bolivia, the aircraft was a popular choice there. Its design was somewhat unconventional, but it enabled it to be flown safely on one engine. The overall performance characteristics were superior to any of its competitors at the time. It was capable of carrying ten passengers, and the United States Navy and Pan American were early customers for it. Three Ju 52/3ms and four W 33/34s completed the fleet.

During this time, LAB offered mainly domestic flights, usually with several stopovers between the departure and destination airports. The stopovers were required because, at that time, all aircraft had a limited range – a situation compounded by operating out of unprepared strips that were often at a high elevation. Additionally, there would often be insufficient passengers to economically operate a point-to-point route network. The route network was centred around two hubs: Cochabamba, which was nominally the operations centre, and Santa Cruz de la Sierra. The one international flight that LAB operated was to Corumbá. Another international flight was available to Arequipa and onwards to Lima in Peru, but this was operated in co-operation with Deutsche Lufthansa Peru. These flights were aimed at the German ex-pat community in that region. The major airports were being upgraded, with a radio-equipped control tower being installed at La Paz's El Alto airport in December 1935.

During these operations, LAB lost two of its Ju 52s. On 17 January 1936, flying between Cochabamba and La Paz, the aircraft, registered as CB-32 and called *Chorolque*, crashed into a swamp northeast of Cochabamba. All those on board, including Jorge Wilstermann, who was just 25, were killed. The second aircraft, registered CB-18, was lost on 15 December 1937 during a flight between La Paz and Apolo. The aircraft crashed near Sorata, a remote area to the north of La Paz, and it was January 1942 before the wreckage was found. The third aircraft, CB-21, remained in service until July 1942, before being sold to Argentina.

In 1937, LAB acquired a Ju 86, which was named *Illimani* after one of the highest mountains in western Bolivia. At the time, it was considered one of the most modern aircraft in the world, though its operational economics were questionable, having seating for just ten passengers and two huge radial engines. No further aircraft of the type were purchased – the Ju 86 was primarily a military aircraft – and the remaining aircraft originally delivered to LAB were later transferred to the FAB. By this time, the German influence at all levels in LAB was significant. Deutsche Lufthansa, as it was known at the time, was anxious to increase its influence in the

A DC-3 carrying the early LAB colour scheme prepares to depart from La Paz. (Folab)

region and was already operating services from Germany to Lima and Rio de Janeiro. There was no direct financial involvement with LAB, but the connections were nevertheless very evident, with support and training being provided directly from Germany, or by Condor Syndikat. LAB's relationships with the two German carriers were useful: both Lufthansa and Condor provided significant feeder services into LAB's routes. Thus, it was possible to fly from Rio de Janeiro to Corumbá by Condor, on to La Paz by LAB and then from La Paz to Lima by Lufthansa Peru. There was no doubt which airline had the more difficult sector of those though, with LAB having to traverse the Andean peaks and additional en-route stops at Roboré, Santa Cruz, Cochabamba and Oruro.

The Gran Chaco War had a devastating effect on Bolivia's economy, and just as it was beginning to slowly recover, World War Two was on the horizon. The US government was becoming increasingly concerned about the German influence and what it saw, by extension, as the potential growth of Naziism throughout South America, and these fears were conveyed to the countries concerned. LAB's board of directors held a meeting in February 1937, which determined that the state should hold 64 per cent of LAB's shares, thus significantly reducing the German shareholding. In fact, the government already owned 60 per cent of the shares, with the remainder made up of about 20 per cent owned by the original shareholders and the balance from contributions made by patriotic Bolivians during the war. The Bolivian government had provided equipment and resources to LAB during the Chaco War, which, according to estimates from the government, allowed for the purchase of two Ju 52s, two Junkers K 43, a metal hangar, engines, tools and other accessories. As a result, LAB owed money to the state. LAB had operated three military versions of the Ju 86K-7 from mid-1938. These were transferred to the FAB in 1940.

Unsurprisingly, the German shareholders were very unhappy about this development. The idea led to a dispute, and the issue was referred to the Bolivian Chamber of Commerce. A year later, the chamber decided that LAB's liability was only 48 per cent of its capital, leaving the remaining 52 per cent to private investors, many of whom were German. To protect their position, the Germans granted the government 48 per cent in Class B shares, without voting rights, while they kept the remaining 52 per cent in Class A shares, which were the only ones with voting rights. At the time, the government did not question the chamber's decision. However, the Supreme Decree of Nationalisation, dated 14 May 1941, did and effectively renounced it, stating, 'The interest of public finances cannot be submitted to arbitration.' Thus, LAB became a nationalised company and the de facto Bolivian flag carrier. The nationalisation was quickly followed by a credit from the US Federal Loan Administration of US$300,000, to be used as working capital and US$454,674 to purchase aircraft. The principal sum, but not the interest, on the loan was paid until 1945, because LAB was not making any profit.

The nationalisation of LAB in May 1941 was the second involving foreign interests in Bolivia; the first had been that of Standard Oil in 1936. The injection of capital allowed LAB to open new routes within the nation. As a result, between 1935 and 1945, LAB was able to increase its network by 2.7 times, achieving 3,712 miles (5,974km), and by 1946, this figure had reached 4,616 miles (7,428km). LAB was concentrating on routes to the east from Cochabamba and Santa Cruz to Trinidad, since these had the highest potential for passengers. The routes to the south of the country took longer to establish, because the southern regions were more thinly populated. One of the principal intentions of the route network was to link the capitals of the nine states that make up Bolivia, and this was not achieved until 1947. Also in 1947, LAB applied for credits directly from the US EXIM Bank in Washington for US$1.5m and then through the government with the American Embassy for US$3m.

Pan American Grace (Panagra)

Headquartered in New York, this company was originally formed as a joint venture between Pan American World Airways and the Grace Shipping Company in 1929. From its beginnings, it had close connections with South America, especially Peru. Both its shipping and air routes stretched down the west coast of South America as far as Chile. Its aim was to compete with SCADTA, a German-owned airline based in Colombia (the forerunner of Avianca), and Panagra held something of a monopoly over routes in the area in the 1940s and 1950s. The company merged with Braniff International in 1967, and as such became the largest US carrier operating in South America.

In 1932, Panagra set up an agreement with LAB for carrying mail. LAB would carry passengers and mail from La Paz to Tacna, a southern Peruvian town near the Pacific coast, and Panagra would carry it from there. However, the agreement only lasted a month – from 27 May to 27 June 1935 – although a contract signed between Panagra and LAB on 3 June 1941 allowed for greater co-operation between the two airlines. On 2 August 1941, Panagra officially took over the operation of LAB, having been given a five-year management services contract, following which the German employees of the airline were made redundant. A loan of US$750,000 was obtained from the US, and Panagra was granted 23 per cent of LAB's shares. By 1944, the shareholding in LAB was as follows: government 53 per cent, Panagra 23 per cent, and private individuals 24 per cent. In addition, Panagra took over the route from Cochabamba to Puerto Suárez. This was an unusual move because routes within a country are known as cabotage routes, meaning that normally only the carrier of that country may operate within its territory, thus protecting it from competition from foreign carriers. The arrangement meant that the points at which the LAB and Panagra routes converged were La Paz, Oruro, Cochabamba and Santa Cruz. At the time, Bolivia and Ecuador were the only two countries that allowed foreign airlines to operate on domestic routes. For its part, Panagra operated between eight airfields in addition to its international service, which operated via La Paz.

In April 1937, Panagra had inaugurated a service between La Paz and Buenos Aires. The first part of the journey was to Salta, with stops in Oruro, Uyuni and Villazón. The aircraft then stayed overnight in Salta and continued to Buenos Aires the following day. As part of the agreement, Panagra was responsible for the construction of the airports in Oruro, Cochabamba and Santa Cruz, together with those in Sucre and Vallegrande. In 1941, for example, the connecting points between the routes of LAB and Panagra were La Paz, Oruro, Cochabamba and Santa Cruz; the airports and other services would be used jointly and the costs would be shared. However, the Bolivian government viewed this only as a temporary concession until its own domestic carriers had developed sufficiently to replace the Panagra services. At that time, two other operators existed: Empresa Transportes Aéreos (ETA), a company later renamed Transportes Aéreos Militar (TAM) under the control of the FAB, and Corporación Boliviana de Fomento (Bolivian Development Corporation) (CBF). Both were government-owned organisations tasked with providing important air links to the less-accessible areas of the country, where a conventional airline service would be uneconomical.

In the case of Cochabamba, Panagra invested in the construction of the airport with a paved runway 5,900ft (1,800m) in length, 190ft (60m) wide and a cross runway 4,921ft (1,500m) long, together with the necessary lighting for night operations. Both LAB and Panagra were sharing the operational costs of the airfields they flew into. In 1948, their competitors – TAM and CBF – were also using the same airfields and facilities but were becoming unhappy about the LAB–Panagra collaboration, and a dispute began over who had control over the airports. TAM and CBF wanted a bigger input into how they were managed, and it was suggested the government take over responsibility for this, but LAB and Panagra strongly objected, and when a joint venture between the interested parties and the government was mooted, it too was rejected, with LAB arguing that there was no one in government with the ability to carry out the function. Panagra felt that the state should become involved, but it was overruled as the lesser partner in the arrangement.

The significance of Panagra taking over cabotage routes can be demonstrated by the following figures. Before LAB was nationalised, Panagra's share of the Bolivian aviation market was 4.6 per cent of the passengers, 3.6 per cent of the mail and only 0.2 per cent of the cargo. This was not the case in 1944 though, when Panagra carried 50 per cent of the passengers, 25 per cent of the mail and 60 per cent of the cargo carried by air. LAB was left to supply the feeder services, but only within Bolivia. However, Panagra's main contribution was in improving and developing airports. Panagra had refurbished the airports it used, such as Oruro in 1937, with a view to more efficient handling of the mail. Oruro Airport was later rebuilt and inaugurated in 1942. Its aircraft were more modern than those of LAB, whose record of accidents peaked in 1941 with the loss of six aircraft. Therefore, it had the support of public opinion and the government. The Panagra support included runways, radio and landline communications and meteorological services. Given the time when this investment was taking place, i.e., during World War Two, it was clear the influence of the US government was instrumental in this move, reflecting the State Department's concern about the growing German influence in Latin America. However, LAB was unhappy about the increasing involvement of Panagra in Bolivia's aviation industry, and after a number of meetings the Panagra shareholding was reduced. In 1944, for example, the shareholding composition was government 53 per cent, individuals 24 per cent and Panagra 23 per cent.

The influence of Panagra in Bolivia, 1932–61.

Year	Event
1932	Agreement with LAB for mail handling. LAB would carry correspondence from La Paz to Tacna before handing over to Panagra. It only lasted from 27 May to 27 December.
1935	18 May: Signing of the decree. The airports would be included in phases. All the infrastructure, landing strips, radios and communication networks, passenger terminals and installation of other parts of airport infrastructure that did not previously exist would be provided by Panagra. 30 May: First radio station in Charaña 31 May: First flight from La Paz to Tacna with passengers and mail December: Radio station installed in La Paz
1936	9 October: Expansion of coverage to Oruro and then to Uyuni 16 October: Radio station in Uyuni 19 October: Radio station in Oruro
1937	12 March: Expansion of the route to Villazón 16 April: First flight from La Paz to Córdoba (Argentina)
1938	October: Two weekly flights between La Paz and Arequipa (Chile)
1942	September: Meteorological station to be installed in Cochabamba for use by Panagra and LAB
1961	1 May: Suspension of internal (cabotage) flights in Bolivia by Panagra

In 1942, LAB reviewed its fleet with a view to disposing of the now ageing Junkers. It bought a used Lockheed 18 Lodestar from Yukon Southern Airways – a Canadian local operator based in Edmonton, in the Canadian state of Alberta. This was an 18-seat twin-engined aircraft, pressurised, with a range of almost 1,500 miles (2,400km). The aircraft, CB-25, was delivered in 1942 but was destroyed in a hangar fire on 21 August 1944. Bolivia was no stranger to revolutions and insurgency, and it was the result of such events that two further aircraft were lost. A second Lodestar, CB-26, had been acquired in 1942 but was later destroyed in an accident near Sucre, when it was shot down by rebels. The third flying example, CB-28, was the target of a similar attack on 29 August 1949. A further aircraft, CB-27, also joined the fleet but was used mainly for spare parts.

When Panagra's first contract expired on 2 August 1946, a second contract was signed, but with reduced participation by Panagra. The management part of the agreement was terminated, while the technical agreement remained. A new contract was signed on 26 November that year. The shareholding was also amended, with Panagra now holding 19.8 per cent, the Bolivian government 55.4 per cent percent and the remainder being private investors.

In 1947, with a view to supporting Bolivia in the development of domestic civil aviation within the country, the US government had established a mission in La Paz. This was a wide-ranging support scheme, in which training for aircraft maintenance, air traffic control and both ground and flight personnel were included. In the process of setting up a fully fledged civil aeronautics department, separate units were formed to deal with the construction of airports, licensing of personnel and accident investigation. Previously, such legislation was in the hands of the FAB.

Chapter 2
1945–60: Recovery from the war and sustained growth

Perhaps surprisingly, given the high level of aviation activity until now, it was not until 1947 that control of civil aviation passed to the civil authorities. Previously, the military had been responsible for all aviation matters. A supreme resolution of 7 August 1948 confirmed the new administration and appointed a new Director General of Civil and Commercial Aeronautics (DGCA), who would be responsible to the Minister of Public Works and Communications.

In 1948, the government increased the shareholding in LAB to 50 million bolivars. With World War Two at an end, this enabled LAB to take advantage of the availability of surplus DC-3s and C-46s, and with an eye to restructuring and increasing its operations, it began to renew the fleet. The first DC-3 arrived in August 1945, followed by a further five aircraft, all having been sold off by the US Army Air Forces. Two more were acquired in 1946, one in 1948 and another in 1950. In total, the airline operated 19 DC-3s. LAB was not alone in purchasing additional aircraft for its fleet. TAM, who until now had been engaged in moving troops and supplies around the country, was now operating in a more civilian role, while CBF, which owned a small fleet of aircraft, was, in effect, competing with LAB over many of these routes.

The meat flying operation

One of the more unusual aspects of the civil aviation scene in Bolivia was the movement of meat from the area known as the Beni to La Paz and the other major cities by air. The rich pasturelands of the area produced excellent beef cattle, but the problem lay in how to move it from there to the more populated Altiplano, which, in the case of La Paz, sits at 11,500ft (3,500m) above it, elevation wise. The significance of this operation should not be underestimated, and since LAB was one of the pioneers of this route, it is worth recounting how it used to work in some detail.

The population of La Paz in the 1950s numbered around 250,000 but, as with many cities in South America, during its more prosperous years, its population grew quickly and, by 1980, one million people were living in Bolivia's principal city. All these people needed to be fed, and since meat is a staple of most South American diets, there was a huge demand for it. Road transport was not an option. There were no refrigerated vehicles, it took too long to travel from the main centre, Trinidad, and in the rainy season the roads were impassable. As long ago as 1952, the amount of meat carried annually on the Beni–La Paz air route reached 5,400 tonnes; moving it by road would have proved a severe logistical challenge, hence the airlift.

LAB saw an opening in the market, and in the early 1950s purchased four B-17s specifically to deal with this. They had been converted for civil use and fitted with cargo doors in the US and being four-engined and designed to carry heavy loads, seemed ideally suited for the purpose. The DC-3s and

C-47 CB-34 was damaged on landing near Pilcomayo on 15 April but was later repaired and returned to service. (Folab)

C-46s that the airline already operated were also used for additional meat-carrying flights. The crews and their aircraft, known as carniceros (butchers), would leave La Paz, usually loaded with essential supplies. The cargo manifest would be a diverse one: generators, building materials, toilet paper, cleaning materials, canned goods, furniture – even beer; all items required in this remote area of the country. These were not promoted as passenger flights – though passengers were not often refused if they offered to pay their way onto these scheduled services. Such flights would be far from comfortable. A few basic canvas seats would be provided, which were secured onto the cargo floor by bolts. There would be no onboard service and often no toilet, depending on the type of aircraft. The cargo would be lashed down very tightly, to obviate the possibility of it moving during the flight and with the juddering of the aircraft during the take-off run.

The thinness of the altitude at La Paz meant that most aircraft used almost the whole 13,325ft (4,061m) runway to get airborne. An engine failure would require an immediate return to the airfield – if they were lucky. The land around the airport would be littered with the carcasses of aircraft that had failed to make it much beyond the airport. Now began the business of negotiating the mountain passes to begin the descent to the Beni. The passes were narrow, and it felt as though the trees could be touched from the window. There was no room for error. Once the mountain ranges had been cleared, the long, slow descent over the jungle into Trinidad would begin. In the early days, there was just a prepared earthen strip for a runway; there was no fencing and animals would frequently roam onto the airfield, so a low pass would be required in order to clear the airfield. Trinidad, while the busiest, was not the only destination. Other airports in the region, though less busy, were Rurrenabaque, San Borja, Reyes and Santa Ana, and also handled the traffic. At the time, most of these were little more than a grass strip with a windsock.

No time would be wasted in unloading the inbound cargo, despite the heat. As the cargo was being unloaded, the cattle were being slaughtered in nearby premises and the loading of the meat would quickly begin. The average daytime temperature in the region would be about 30°C, so the loading had to take place as quickly as possible. So fresh was the meat that blood would still be dripping from it as it was loaded onto the aircraft. Most of this would disappear down a basic drainage hole drilled into the rear floor of the aircraft. The fresh meat attracted an enormous number of flies, whose attention could only be distracted by placing a recently severed head of one of the beasts inside the aircraft. As soon as the loading had been completed, and the cargo lashed down with ropes, the door would be closed and the aircraft would taxi out for take-off. The weight and balance (the way the aircraft is loaded for optimum flying conditions) of the aircraft was not a primary consideration – the meat was not weighed before loading – and there is no doubt that many of the flights would have been operated outside what would normally be considered a safe operating envelope. A typical load

An early photo from El Alto Airport in La Paz, as a C-47 taxies in. (LAB)

A shaft of strong Bolivian sunlight highlights CP-568 at La Paz. (Folab)

would vary between 4.5 and 5 tonnes. The market price for fresh meat during the time was up to six times higher in La Paz, so while the cost of flying it added a considerable increase to the price, the economics made sense and, thus, there was a temptation to overload the aircraft.

The next problem to be faced by the crews was traversing the Andes to reach La Paz or one of the other major cities. The aircraft were unpressurised, and the flying would necessarily be done at heights at which oxygen was severely depleted, so they would supplement their oxygen supply by breathing from a tube attached to an oxygen bottle, usually the type used by scuba divers. Turbulence, brought about by the winds swirling around the mountain peaks, was common. The crews often looked like the cast from a World War Two film, wearing large bomber jackets and heavy boots to combat the cold. A typical flight would take about 90 minutes, depending on weather conditions. Another comparison with World War Two was the means of navigation. The aircraft did not carry radar, and there was no way of knowing the weather conditions until they were airborne. The pilots would navigate using their watches and compasses to thread their way through the peaks, which were often covered in cloud.

Once safely landed at their destination, another process would begin. La Paz's El Alto airport was vast and a part of the plain on which the airport sits was dedicated to the carniceros. The aircraft would simply park wherever they could on the remote side of the airfield; for the bigger companies, there would be an adobe hut from which the operation would be overseen. Maintenance would usually be carried out as and when required, rather than on a planned basis, usually in the open air or maybe under a basic shelter. The carriage of meat by air was a very competitive business because of the cost–demand ratio and there were many different operators and aircraft operating this service, so overheads were kept to an absolute minimum. During the years of the meat flights, it was not unusual for an aircraft to be involved in an incident or accident almost every month, sometimes even more frequently.

The side of the airport used by the carniceros would be served only by rudimentary roads, and the aircraft would park not on concrete or tarmac but on the available flat earth, populated with grass and weeds. Small huts, actually houses where the 'mecanicos' and their families lived, dotted the landscape and the aircraft taxied to these areas. There were no fences, and the vehicles would assemble immediately to take away the meat as quickly as possible. The cow's head, which had accompanied the flight, would immediately be thrown out onto the dry earth, where the local dogs would quickly arrive to devour what was left, unworried by the flies. If all went well, the meat would be in the market within three hours. Within half an hour, the aircraft would be emptied and hosed down, and if there was cargo for the return trip, it would be loaded. Typically, the aircraft and crews would fly four of these sectors per day. The most common types in use, apart from the B-17s, were the C-46s and DC-3s, all of which were part of LAB's fleet, most of them bought cheaply. Some of the other operators would be using similar aircraft, which would by now be with their fourth or fifth operator. Many of the companies would have just one or two aircraft. Any aircraft that crashed would be quickly stripped of all useable items by the owners, to be stored for spare parts. Arduous and unpleasant as the operating conditions were, there was never any shortage of crews or aircraft for the operation. During the 1970s and 1980s, there were more than 30 different registered operators, most of them involved solely in the meat-carrying business.

At the turn of the century, the meat-carrying business began to wind down. New roads had been opened that were passable all year round. Large, refrigerated trucks were now able to carry the meat to the principal cities, and although the journey typically takes nine hours from Trinidad to La Paz, the costs are significantly cheaper and the meat still arrives in prime condition. Of the aircraft and operators, there is little left. The best known of these, mainly for operating the former LAB B-17s right up until the mid-1980s, was Frigorifico Reyes, which ceased operations in 1994 after 34 years. A few airframe carcasses still litter the far side of El Alto awaiting the scrapman, but the days of the prop-driven meat-haulers are long gone.

In fact, LAB's participation in this industry was relatively short-lived. It was claimed that LAB were charging too much for carrying the meat, so the government encouraged its two main competitors, TAM and CBF, to compete for the route. Other independent carriers, often with just a single aircraft, had become involved in this lucrative business, and eventually LAB pulled out of this operation and left it to smaller independent operators.

The Bolivian Revolution

Bolivia has seen many revolutions in its time, but the one which began in April 1952 was probably the most far-reaching. The leader at the time was General José Ballivián, who had come to power after the previous government refused to stand down after the winner of the 1951 election, Victor Paz Estenssoro, who represented the Movimiento Nacionalista Revoultionario (MNR) party, had been democratically elected. The MNR had stronger support than had previously been the case in most Bolivian coups d'état. Militias of armed workers formed and attacked the army, which consisted mainly of conscripts who were not willing to fight. The army surrendered and Bolivia was in the hands of a radical political movement with popular support and legitimacy, having won the

C-47 CP-735 ended its service life at Cochabamba in June 1975 but continued with other operators until it was written off on 19 October 1990. (Werner Fishdick)

last election. They invited Ángel Paz Estenssoro, whose 1951 election victory had been neutralised by a military coup, to become president. Once in power, the MNR nationalised the tin mines and had plans to redistribute the land.

As might be imagined, the US government, while not entirely in favour of developments, at least appreciated that it was a return to a form of civilian control, on the basis that it was far more acceptable than the Marxist government that had been in control after 1946; though the exchange value of the peso, Bolivia's currency at that time, went from 60 to 12,000 to the dollar between 1952 and 1956. The government, despite its socialist origins, had now begun to look to the US for co-operation which, as a result, had given the US influence over Bolivia's economy. Following pressure from the US, the Bolivian government agreed to compensate the owners of the tin mines and also to introduce an amendment to a previous law, allowing the US to reinvest in Bolivian oil. After 1952, the US sent aid to Bolivia amounting to US$368 million between 1953 and 1964. This was the highest per capita amount ever granted to a Latin American country during those years.

On 6 June 1950, the Bolivian government increased the net capital of LAB, thus passing the majority ownership to the government and subsequently allowing LAB to purchase further aircraft. In an effort to rebuild the airline, the capital shareholding was increased to 50 million bolivars by the Bolivian government in 1948, which enabled LAB to begin rebuilding. This began in 1950 with the purchase of no less than 11 B-17s, but not initially for passenger work. The idea was that being four-engined and used to carrying a heavy bomb load, they would be eminently suitable for carrying large amounts of cargo around the country. However, the arduous operating conditions took their toll: within nine years, five aircraft had been written off. By the mid-1960s, just three aircraft were left in the fleet, and the two remaining aircraft in 1970 were sold.

Along with the B-17s, LAB purchased eight C-46s in 1949. These aircraft were fitted with up to 26 seats, although they were more commonly used as cargo aircraft. The C-46 had acquired a good reputation following its activities in Asia, having flown over the Himalayas in what was known as 'The Hump' between India and China to support the Chinese Army's defence against the invading Japanese. The belief was that if the aircraft could handle the Himalayas, it could do the same in and around the Andes. The background, however, was less reassuring. The C-46 had been rushed into service during World War Two, without the usual preliminaries of rigorous flight testing. Not least of its problems was its 'engine out' performance, which meant that should the aircraft lose an engine at a critical stage of flight, it more often than not resulted in an accident. In the event, just one C-46 was left in LAB service by the mid-1960s, having been outlasted by the B-17s.

LAB was supported by the state, and this support took three different forms. The first was direct aid by way of financing, with capital contributions, together with subsidies and credits. There was also the provision of meteorological services, an important function in a country with terrain and variable weather such as that found in Bolivia. Airfields were maintained by the state. Although this is a common practice, with LAB's extensive route network, it was very important to have reliable airfields

Another view of CP-735. The large freight door allowed it to have a dual role. (Christian Volpati)

into which to operate. However, while the financial support was continuous, the support for runways and meteorological services was more sporadic.

Between 1951 and 1965, a further 11 DC-3s arrived. These later aircraft had been sourced from the used aircraft market. Soon after the arrival of the first DC-3s, a number of C-46s were also received. Some were intended for passenger services, often with cargo on board as well, but because of their rugged structure, they were used for cargo on the routes where airfields were undeveloped; in which case, passenger seats would be fitted. Their prime use was to transport much-needed supplies from the major cities to the lowlands. The aircraft would not normally be heavily loaded when they left La Paz, which was fortuitous, because it is unlikely that, given the thin air at 13,000ft, they would have become airborne with anything like a full load.

During this time, a number of other competitor airlines had appeared on the scene, particularly in respect to the meat traffic. LAB argued that these companies were using what LAB saw as their airports, but for which the airline was not receiving any revenue. The government was unsympathetic, responding that the carrier was, in effect, receiving a government subvention for the provision of services to the Beni and Pando regions in the sparsely populated north, but even this had been overspent by LAB to the amount of US$800,000 in 1960.

One of the problems faced by LAB in the 1950s and '60s was considerable overstaffing. In 1952, the staff had increased from 890 to 1,016 employees and continued to rise until it peaked at 1,511 in 1957. With the fleet at that time standing at 18, it worked out at 84 employees per aircraft. Just a year

A typical Bolivian airport scene of the 1960s. The aircraft is CP-581. (Folab)

A DC-3 is loaded at one of the many remote airfields in Bolivia. (Folab)

later, the overall staffing figure had decreased somewhat to 1,012, but this had corresponded with a decrease in flight hours. This was gradually reduced further to 980 employees by 1960. The reason for the overemployment can be traced to the unionisation of LAB. The Bolivian Revolution had put both the unions and the workers in a much stronger position regarding salaries and employment, and the government was in no position to argue. Any significant argument with the government could result in a strike by one group or other of the employees, thus draining LAB's dwindling finances even further. The then-president of LAB cited what he called 'Union dictatorship' and the operation of financially unviable routes to the east of the country as reasons for LAB's parlous financial state.

In 1950, LAB was awarded the prestigious Order of the Condor of the Andes by the government. The airline now set about improving its domestic network and in 1951 reached an agreement with the Brazilian carrier Cruzeiro do Sul, which had become the successor to Condor Syndikat, to operate services westwards to Corumbá. This also complemented the Panagra service. This triumvirate continued for a few years until, on 19 November 1959, Panagra withdrew its eastbound

This DC-3, CP-583, left LAB's fleet in 1979 and is seen here abandoned in Trinidad after it was seized by the authorities in 1990 on suspicion of drug trafficking. (Robert Domandl)

flights operating from Santa Cruz. In the meantime, LAB had been operating a DC-3 service from Cochabamba to Puerto Suárez, a city in the southeast of Bolivia, on the border with Brazil, while Cruzeiro do Sul continued to serve Corumbá from Santa Cruz.

With a successful domestic operation now in place, LAB began to look at other routes within Latin America. With an inaugural flight on 20 March 1954, the route network was extended to Arica, a major port city in northern Chile. This was a significant milestone for LAB and Bolivia, since it had been agreed that, following the signing of the Treaty of Valparaiso in 1884, Bolivia would, albeit very reluctantly, give up its Pacific coastline. In the Treaty of Peace and Friendship in 1904, Chile had agreed to build a railway line between Arica and La Paz, together with freedom of transit for all goods of Bolivian origin, but this had never worked to its full capability. A short-term agreement had been negotiated with the otherwise unconnected Lloyd Aéreo Colombiano in November 1955, with the aim of operating a service from Bogotá, the Colombian capital, to Cochabamba via Riberalta, but the service lasted only seven months and did nothing to bolster LAB's finances.

In 1956, a stabilisation plan was introduced by the government to try to control inflation. As governments worldwide have discovered, such fiscal measures often do more damage than the inflation

Two B-17s sit outside LAB's maintenance centre in Cochabamba. (Folab)

they were designed to control, and Bolivia was no exception. The plan had several effects on LAB, bringing about a significant loss of revenue. First there was a decrease in air traffic of about 40 per cent because fares had been increased; then the amount of cargo carried decreased, this time to the order of 75 per cent, for the same reason. The most significant of these, however, was an increase in the price of fuel, which accounted for about 30 per cent of LAB's operating costs.

In 1955, two DC-4s were added to the fleet, and Corumbá began to be served by a direct flight in July 1957, with an additional flight to Porto Velho, a Brazilian town to the north of Bolivia in January 1958. A more distant destination, the Paraguayan capital of Asunción, was served by a DC-4 between 1958 and 1959, but the DC-4s were mainly used on busier routes between La Paz, Cochabamba and Santa Cruz. On 2 July 1959, LAB inaugurated a service to Buenos Aires, and, following the arrival of four DC-6Bs in 1960, the first pressurised aircraft to be operated by LAB, another new route was opened to Lima in March 1961. By May 1963, these aircraft also began to fly to the Brazilian commercial centre of São Paulo. This marked a considerable expansion of its international routes, but ones which were not added to for many years.

CP-686 was one of 12 B-17s operated by LAB. It was written off at Trinidad on 4 November 1965. (Folab)

One of the two DC-6Bs owned by LAB, CP-740 ended its life at El Alto. (Richard Vandervord)

A huge crowd greets the arrival of LABs first DC-6B, CP-698, when it arrived at La Paz on 15 December 1960. (Folab)

A view of one of LAB's earlier colour schemes, taken at La Paz in the mid-1950s. The aircraft remained in service until 1961, when it was sold. (Jennifer Gradidge/edcoatescollection.com)

Chapter 3
1960–70: Difficult times

By 1958, LAB was recording significant losses, to the extent that, during the first half of the 1960s, the airline required outside help. Finally, the government provided loans to LAB through the Central Bank of Bolivia in several tranches to enable the airline to purchase spare parts and fuel. In March 1960, Panagra still held a 20 per cent shareholding in LAB, with the Bolivian government holding the remaining the majority share. The fleet consisted of seven DC-3s, a DC-4 and six Boeing B-17s. A single Lockheed Electra II would join the fleet in August 1968. Nevertheless, the 1960s became increasingly difficult for LAB, with the need for foreign exchange to purchase spare parts, fuel and pay for the insurance of the aircraft. This put LAB constantly on the brink of suspending operations.

By this time, Santa Cruz had replaced Cochabamba as the largest hub for LAB's operations with another important regional hub at Trinidad airport. It had also become the maintenance base. In 1963, the Panagra contract was finally terminated. Now LAB faced a number of serious problems. Because of crashes and other accidents in which aircraft were written off, and the inability to properly maintain the aircraft that were airworthy, the airline was unable to run a proper scheduled service. The fact that a number of independent airlines had sprung up in Bolivia since the end of World War Two did not help. The reduction in the airline's schedules meant less income, leading to a shortage of funds to deal with these problems.

Despite this, the route network continued to expand and covered most useable airports in the country. In 1964, the fleet comprised DC-3s, DC-6s and B-17s. The B-17s were used to bring the meat from Trinidad since, being a former World War Two bomber, it was powerful and capable of carrying heavy loads. Although it was officially a freighter, it is known that passengers were occasionally carried on the service. The route expansion was helped by the fact that since 1936, when the government had nationalised it, Yacimientos Petrolíferos Fiscales Bolivianos (YPFB, Bolivian Fiscal Oil Deposits), the Bolivian state petroleum company, agreed to cut the cost of aviation fuel for LAB. In 1964, YPFB, reduced the cost of fuel to LAB by 20 per cent, to help it with financial difficulties. One of the other ways in which the government helped LAB was by exempting them from taxes on imported goods, such as aircraft and the support equipment such as spare engines, associated with them. Some of this was brought in by rail and LAB was allowed to pay reduced carriage rates to the state railway company.

In 1968, LAB obtained a credit line, with government backing, for the purchase of a Boeing 727-100 and two Fairchild F-27s. Thus, LAB was able to augment its network and provide connecting flights to the international routes operated by the Boeing 727. Further aircraft were purchased or leased, depending on requirements.

Coupled with this was the appearance of competitor airlines, which offered unscheduled routes at cheaper fares. LAB was not in a position to buy new equipment and had begun negotiations with the US Agency for International Development (USAID) in 1959. The negotiations did not proceed easily, and it was not until the mid-1960s that the money was received by LAB. Together with this, a

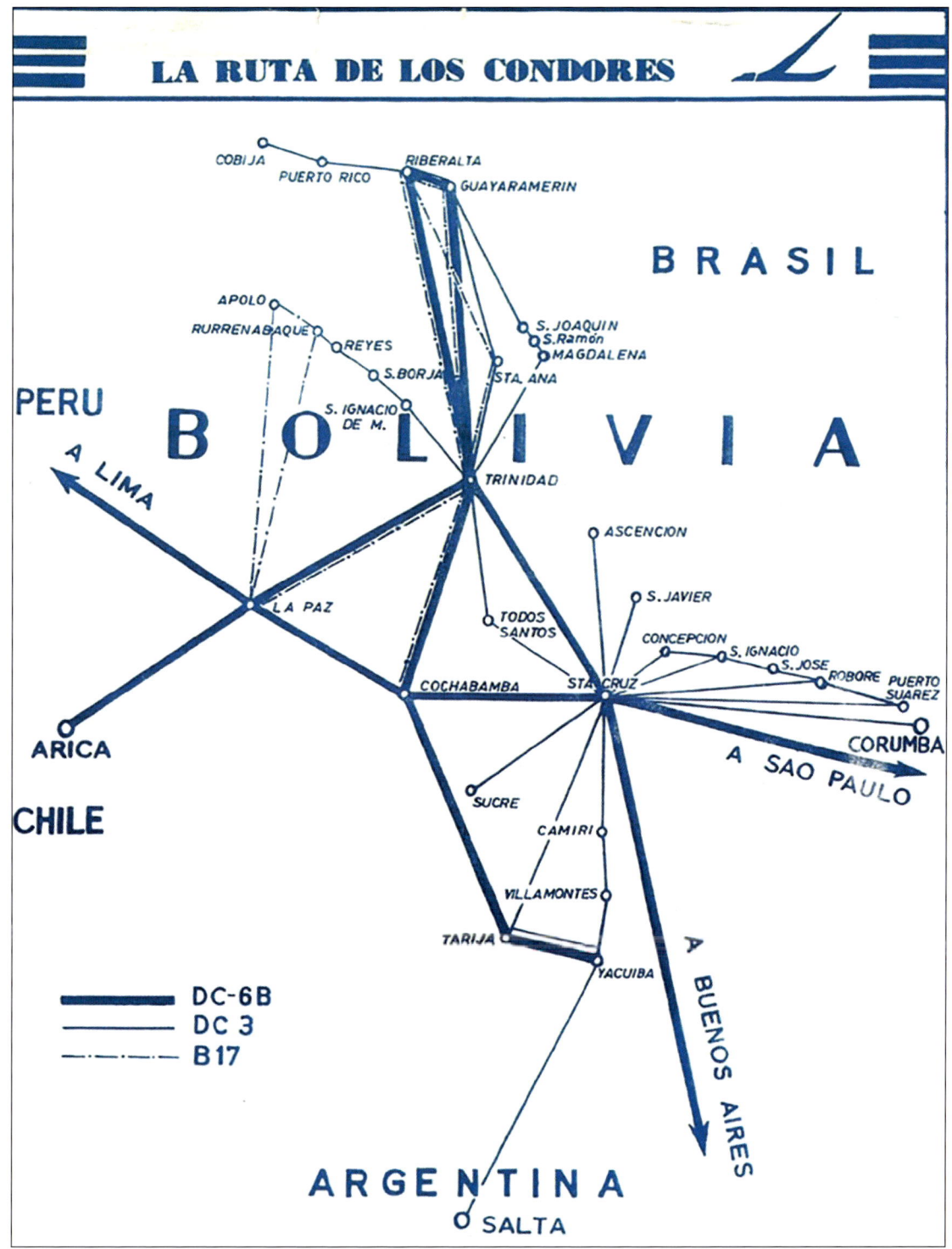
The LAB route network in 1964. (Bjorn Larsson/timetableimages.com)

Minneapolis-based US carrier called North Central Airlines, which had a significant domestic network, was given a contract by USAID as part of a package to provide managerial and technical assistance for a two-year period. The negotiation itself took over a year to complete. Following this, a company known as Systems Analysis Research Corporation (SARC), based in Washington, DC, was called in to advise on new equipment. Despite having had the Handley Page Dart Herald and the HS 748 demonstrated to them, SARC persuaded LAB that the most suitable aircraft would be the Fairchild F-27, a version of the Fokker F-27, built under licence in the US. The aircraft would be fitted with 36 seats and replace the lone Electra II on what would become an extended domestic network.

The lone Electra

It is unusual for an airline to operate just one aircraft of a particular type. Such an operation brings with it the need for specialised crewing, operations and maintenance, but in the case of LAB it is worth examining the reasons in greater detail. The Electra was bought from American Airlines and was eight years old when LAB received it on 12 August 1968. It was registered as CP-853. The Electra was the first, and one of the very few, turbine-engined airliners to be built in the US. The fact that only 170 were built perhaps has more to do with the arrival of the competition, the Boeing 727, 737 and the Douglas DC-9, soon afterwards. In its initial service life, the Electra had acquired a bad reputation, with nine accidents occurring within three years of its initial operation. It should be added, however,

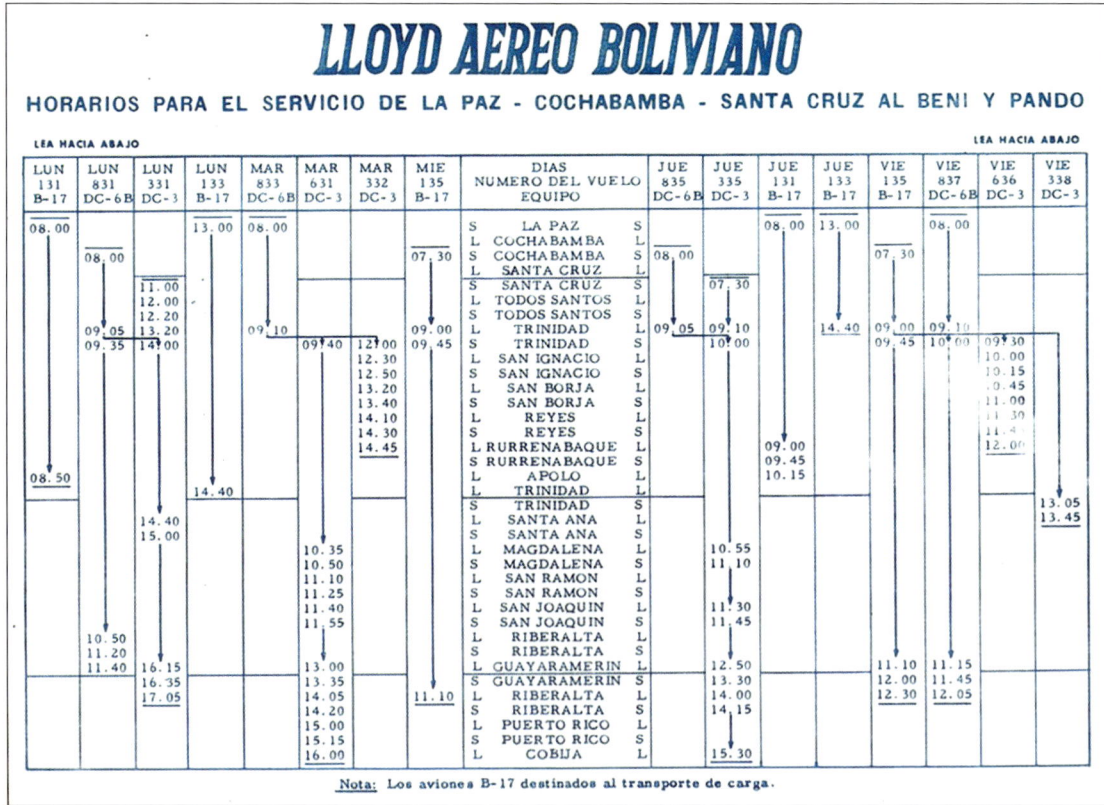

The LAB domestic timetable for the same period. Note that the B-17 appears on the schedule. (Bjorn Larsson/timetableimages.com)

An advertisement showing LAB's international and domestic routes. (LAB)

that these were not always caused by failures of the aircraft itself; it was known to require a significant amount of maintenance, which increased the likelihood of poor maintenance practices and shortcuts.

With a cruising speed of 373mph, (600km/h) and a typical range of 2,200 miles (3,500km), it was ideally suited for short- and medium-haul flights. In the case of LAB, it had been fitted with comfortable seats and a larger, more useful galley, having 17 seats in first class and 54 seats in economy. Passengers who had been used to the piston-engined aircraft of the day found it very pleasant. The choice of the Electra by LAB was quite possibly influenced by the fact that Varig in Brazil and Ecuatoriana in Ecuador were both operating the type. The aircraft was used on both domestic and international services. The route to Buenos Aires, for example, would take it from La Paz via Santa Cruz to Buenos Aires. On another occasion, it would start from Peru's capital, Lima, and operate via La Paz, Cochabamba and Santa Cruz to São Paulo. At this time, DC-6s would also be used on the international routes, while the DC-3s would be operated on the domestic services. Once the first Boeing 727 arrived in 1970, the Electra took over more of the domestic routes and was used as a standby aircraft. In January 1974, it was transferred to the transport division of the FAB, with whom it remained until 2015, when it was repainted TAM-69 and later taken out of service and put into storage.

In the 1960s, Santa Cruz replaced Cochabamba as the main hub for LAB's operations, and the airport at Trinidad had now become a hub for the eastern region. La Paz handled the international routes and connections were available throughout the country, although most of these involved several intermediate stops. During the 1970s, LAB's president, Mario Patino Ayoroa, made a point of developing the carrier's international routes, meaning that LAB was now able to offer flights to Argentina, Chile and Peru. The shorter routes were served by DC-3s, while the longer international flights were served by DC-6s. Scheduled services to the US were also inaugurated.

October 1976 saw LAB receive its first Boeing 707 – an aircraft sub-leased from Rodel Leasing, based in Texas. This was a -131C series aircraft, originally delivered to Trans World Airlines, and the

LAB's only Electra CP-853 is seen being serviced during a turnaround in Cochabamba. (Folab)

first Boeing 707 production variant. LAB had recognised that, because of its geographical position in South America, and given the problems of using surface transport for moving goods around, there was an increasing demand for cargo to be moved by air. This aircraft, registered N730JP, was fitted with a large freight door in the forward fuselage, thus enabling it to be operated in a combi – part passenger, part cargo – configuration. This suited LAB's operation very well, since the load factors on the international flights were not always very economic. Unfortunately, this aircraft was only in service for a short time with LAB. Having been delivered in early October, it was written off just a few weeks later in a catastrophic accident near Santa Cruz airport while operating a cargo flight from Santa Cruz to Miami. A replacement aircraft, this time a -323C series, arrived in September 1977. In August 1991, it was written off in a hangar fire at Dothan, Alabama, while being repainted. The third Boeing 707, also a -323C, was received in June 1981. Both these aircraft were formerly owned by American Airlines.

By March 1990, the airline was employing about 1,700 people and was owned by the government, except for a nominal 0.02 per cent private shareholding. The route network comprised 21 domestic and 15 international destinations, including Brazil, Chile, Panama, Peru and Venezuela. Some of these countries were used as en route stopovers. The fleet was now made up of two Boeing 707-320Cs (combi versions), three Boeing 727-200s, two Boeing 727-100s, a Fokker F-27-600 and a Fokker F-27 -200. It was during this year that LAB moved its main hub in Santa Cruz from El Trompillo Airport to Viru Viru International Airport. El Trompillo (the trumpet) is the ultimate downtown airport, being just 1¼ miles (2km) from the city centre. Despite its 9,144ft (2,787m) runway, a lack of planning control had allowed it to become surrounded by buildings, and thus there was no room for LAB to expand

After service with LAB, CP-853 was transferred to the FAB. (aussieairliners.com)

This anonymous F-27 is actually CP-2013 and was donated to LAB by the Netherlands government. (Robert Domandl)

its operations. Viru Viru is located about 10 miles (16km) northeast of Santa Cruz and was opened in 1985. It has an 11,483ft (3,500m) runway. It sits at the comparatively low elevation of 1,225ft (373m) and is capable of handling a Boeing 747-400; it is now the busiest airport in Bolivia. The much lower elevation means that full loads can be carried from the airport on longer routes.

When the Bolivian government decided to put LAB shares up for sale in 1995, international bidders took a careful look at LAB and its operations, and, of these, only the Brazilian airline VASP, itself privatised in 1990 and based in São Paulo, bid. On 1 December 1995, control of LAB was handed over to VASP at its headquarters in Cochabamba. VASP did not just sit on the shares, however; it invested in LAB. In 2002, the maintenance base at Santa Cruz was further developed: a building to house spare parts was constructed and the main hangar extended. The maintenance facilities were inspected and approved by the US Federal Aviation Administration, together with Boeing, thus enabling LAB to undertake major maintenance of both airframes and engines to the highest level, not only for itself but also for third parties. In October 2002, Avensa of Venezuela became the first third-party carrier to have an aircraft, one of its Boeing 727-200s, overhauled there. LAB was the only Andean Pact country allowed to do this. A centralised reservations system was also set up. By this time, LAB was flying to 26 destinations with 45 daily flights and carrying about 1.3 million passengers per year.

This F-27A was leased from French carrier TAT by LAB between January 1985 and August 1987. (Folab)

Chapter 4

1970–90: Steady growth

A more positive development was the arrival of LAB's first jet, a Boeing 727-100 series on 17 February 1970. The aircraft was registered CP-861 and had been delivered direct from Boeing, configured with 119 economy-class seats. On 14 March 1970, following permission obtained from Argentina, LAB operated its first Boeing 727 flight from Santa Cruz to Buenos Aires in two and a half hours, clipping 40 minutes off the time taken by the Electra on the same route. And, more importantly, it was able to carry 42 more passengers on each flight than the turboprop. At the same time, the DC-3 was being withdrawn and replaced by the Fokker F-27J. This left the Electra in an unusual situation, being too big for the domestic routes and too small and slow for the international routes.

The Boeing was quickly put onto the Cochabamba–La Paz service and was joined by two more -100 series aircraft, one in 1974 and one in 1975. A further purchase in 1975 was the first -200 series, also received direct from Boeing. A further -100 series was leased between March 1977 and August 1978, until a new -200 series was delivered from Boeing in 1978. A second -200 series was delivered in October 1978. The 727 fleet now enabled LAB to run a full international service, from Miami in the north to Santiago in the south. Previously, LAB had to send its Boeings to the US for major maintenance checks, but with its newly approved Santa Cruz maintenance base, LAB was now permitted to perform maintenance up to Check D level (complete major overhaul), thus enabling the airline to make significant savings in foreign currency, as everything could bought and paid for in the local currency.

LAB had three principal bases. Some of the management was based at La Paz, but Cochabamba was the main administrative centre. The third city in the trio was Santa Cruz. This was the city where all LAB's maintenance was carried out. The city is significantly lower, at a mere 1,300ft (400m), which is why it was chosen as the maintenance base – because carrying out general maintenance checks and calibrating aircraft engines at high altitudes is a difficult task.

CP-1070 was acquired from Braniff in September 1974. (Folab)

Anuncian su tarifa conjunta de

USD 838.00

(en pesos mexicanos al tipo del cambio del día)

A

LA PAZ - BOLIVIA COCHABAMBA Y STA. CRUZ.

VIA **PANAMA**

Consulte su agente de viajes amigo o a:

AIR PANAMA
MEXICO, D.F., MEXICO
Paseo de la Reforma No. 116 P.B.
06600 México, D.F.
Tels: 566-6860, 566-7557, 566-7568

MONTERREY, N.L. MEXICO
Ave. Hidalgo No. 922 Pte. Letra "G"
Telex: 038-30-24
Tels. 44-8291, 44-8238

LLOYD AEREO BOLIVIANO
DISTRITO FEDERAL
Reforma No. 133, P. B. Local B
México, D.F.
Tels.: 546-4638 y 592-7408

A copy of an advertisement issued in Mexico by LAB, in conjunction with Air Panama, for its service from Panama to Bolivia. (LAB)

One of the two DC-6Bs, CP-707, was lost with all on board, on 15 March 1963, while on a flight from Arica in Chile to La Paz. However, on 26 September 1969, Bolivia suffered its worst aviation accident when an LAB DC-6B, CP-698, en route from Santa Cruz to La Paz, crashed into a mountain at an altitude of 15,500ft (4,724m), 110 miles (176km) southeast of La Paz. All 74 on board were killed, including the players and staff of one of Bolivia's major football teams. So remote was the location that the wreckage was not found for three days. The Andes had claimed yet another victim.

Soon afterwards, the new aircraft was used on international flights to Arica, São Paulo and Buenos Aires. The Boeing 727 proved to be a good fit for LAB's route structure, both on the domestic and international routes, and its reliability was a bonus.

Despite this success, the problem of La Paz's altitude remained a thorn in the side of LAB's operations. Until now, LAB had circumvented the problem by routing the longer-haul flights through Santa Cruz. The airport's relatively low altitude meant that the 727, an aircraft not really designed for longer-haul operations, could take off fully loaded with the engines operating at maximum power and, with an en-route stop in Panama, could fly to Miami, for example. When the Boeing 727-200 was announced, LAB ordered two of the type. The more powerful Pratt & Whitney JT8D-17R engines allowed them to operate directly from La Paz, and they were put into service in December 1977. The airline now operated five Boeing 727s and was able to expand its route network to include Manaus and Caracas. In January 1978, Cali in Colombia was added to the network. With the Boeings performing the longer-haul routes and the F-27s taking care of the domestic network, LAB now had a comprehensive route structure in place, serving 20 destinations within Bolivia and offering useful connecting services, thus producing significant revenue for the carrier.

CP-1116 undergoes a major check at LAB's maintenance base at Cochabamba in 1992. (Gerry Manning)

Another view of CP-1116. Note the basic equipment being used. (Gerry Manning)

CP-2013 was donated to LAB by the Netherlands government and later transferred to the FAB. (Robert Domandl)

CP-861, sporting the last LAB colour scheme, arrives at La Paz. (Robert Domandl)

CP-1070 was bought from Braniff in 1974 and is seen withdrawn from use in Cochabamba. (Robert Domandl)

1970–90: Steady growth

Another aircraft withdrawn from use in Cochabamba. This time a -200 series, CP-1367. (Robert Domandl)

A trio of Boeing 727s withdrawn from use at Cochabamba. (Robert Domandl)

Seen operating the scheduled service into Miami is CP-1276. (Michael Prophet)

The same aircraft, in the more modern scheme, is towed to the terminal building in Cochabamba. (Richard Domandl)

1970–90: Steady growth

La Paz's El Alto Airport is the background for CP-1367 during a turnaround. (Chris Mak)

CP-1223 withdrawn from use at Cochabamba. (Robert Domandl)

Another view of CP-1223 at Cochabamba. (Michael Prophet)

Lying where it originally crashed, just short of the runway at Trinidad, but stripped of all useful parts, is CP-2429. (Robert Domandl)

The interior of CP-2429, now covered by overgrown jungle. (Robert Domandl)

Following the demise of LAB, CP-2464 was transferred to Aerosur, which later went bankrupt. (Robert Domandl)

Another view, showing the striking colour scheme adopted by AeroSur. (Robert Domandl)

Allegro Airways was based in Mexico, but this aircraft, CP-2427, was operated on a lease by LAB. (Robert Domandl)

CP-1367 wears the VASP-inspired colour scheme following the takeover. (Gerry Manning)

The pristine manoeuvring areas at Miami are in sharp contrast to those in Bolivia, as CP-1367 is towed onto the stand. (Michael Prophet)

CP-861 arrives at Cochabamba in 2005. (Michael Prophet)

The forward end of CP-1223, also at Cochabamba. (Michael Prophet)

The halcyon days of LAB, with four Boeing 727s lined up outside the terminal. (Folab)

Asunción, Paraguay, is the scene for this image of CP-1223. (Helio Bastos Salmon)

CP-1276 looking distinctly abandoned at Cochabamba. (Robert Domandl)

CP-1276, seen from another angle, as it is towed onto stand at Cochabamba. (Bob O' Brien Collection)

The registration has been painted out on this -100 series, which was withdrawn from use at Cochabamba. (Michael Prophet)

Major maintenance is taking place on this -200 series at Cochabamba in this 2005 image. (Michael Prophet)

CP-861 is shown here in the original LAB colour scheme. (Gerry Manning)

CP-1276 sits at the maintenance area in Miami. (Gerry Manning)

CP-1276 had winglets fitted in 2004. (Gerry Manning)

The clean lines of the Boeing 727 are evident in this image. (Gerry Manning)

The proximity of the Andes is clear from this image of CP-861. (Richard Domandl)

Cochabamba Airport is the backdrop as CP-861 arrives. (Michael Prophet)

CP-1223 during a major overhaul at Cochabamba. (Gerry Manning)

CP-861 prepares for departure at La Paz.

Another image of CP-681 preparing for departure at Cochabamba. (Gerry Manning)

This aircraft, parked outside at Cochabamba, is believed to be CP-1070. (Robert Domandl)

A 2005 image of a -200 series 727 at Cochabamba. (Michael Prophet)

CP-1223 lies outside the maintenance centre in Cochabamba awaiting its fate. (Michael Prophet)

Another view of CP-1223. (Michael Prophet)

CP-1367 completes another flight on the LAB schedule. (Folab)

CP-1266, complete with winglets, outside the main Cochabamba maintenance base. (Michael Prophet)

Chapter 5

1990–2007

From the early months of 1994, LAB began to experience increasing financial difficulties, despite operating a comprehensive network of scheduled domestic and international services, including the principal South American capitals, the eastern US, Cuba, Mexico and Madrid – its sole European destination. The government, increasingly concerned by this development, began to negotiate with potential buyers to prepare for the privatisation of the airline. Although the Brazilian airline VASP showed considerable interest in investing in LAB, there had been something of a scandal surrounding VASP prior to the takeover. Wagner Canhedo, the company's president, had received US$53m in 1990 from the state government of São Paulo, just days before acquiring VASP for US$45m. In 1995, it acquired a 50 per cent holding in LAB.

During the government of Gonzalo Sánchez de Lozada, the sale of LAB's shares took place on 19 October 1995. The terms were such that 50 per cent of the package was priced at 90 per cent less

CP-1698 seen here parked at Cochabamba. (Bob O'Brien Collection)

Ex-American Airlines 707-323C CP-1698 being towed at Miami. (Michael Prophet)

than LAB's true value. Ultimately, this meant that when the deal went through the following year, all liabilities, totalling US$350m, had to be absorbed by the Central Bank of Bolivia. Thus, Wagner Canhedo had knowingly conducted a fraudulent transaction.

VASP then set about merging the two airlines, starting with a common colour scheme and a frequent-flyer programme. By July 1998, 50 per cent of the shares were held by VASP, with 48.3 per cent belonging to the Bolivian government and the remainder owned by private investors. For reasons that were never fully explained, the transfer of shares to Bolivian citizens never took place. Instead, they were transferred en bloc to the country's two pension fund insurers: Futoro de Bolivia and Banco Bilbao Vizcaya (BBV) Forecast. However, VASP's tenure of LAB was to be short-lived because the investing airline ran into financial difficulties of its own and was forced to sell back its shares to Bolivian investors in 2001.

Later, in 2004, LAB acquired shares in Ecuatoriana de Aviación – the national airline of Ecuador at that time. This was in compensation for outstanding debts owed to LAB and led to a codeshare between the two carriers. This did little to help LAB though, because Ecuatoriana was in a poor financial condition itself.

Colour schemes

VASP's influence was sufficient to persuade LAB to change its colour scheme, which in fact was a clone of that used by VASP. This was changed again in 2004, when LAB introduced a new corporate image. The pale blue, which had formed part of the original colour scheme since 1996 was abandoned in favour of a darker blue. To contrast with this, a yellow edge was added. It was considered that this would give the carrier a more modern image.

In 2001, Ernesto B. Asbún, a former LAB pilot and the owner of a major Bolivian TV station, bought the stocks back from VASP. This was not straightforward, because the shares that VASP sold were then appropriated by the state to cover outstanding debts that were owed, but finally an agreement was reached on the situation. Because the former owners of VASP were involved, and there are strict rules on foreign investment in Bolivia, a series of claims and counterclaims followed, which were argued through the courts. Asbún did not normally make large investments, but he was able to capitalise the debts Ecuatoriana had contracted with Lloyd during the management of VASP. Thus, he also bought 51 per cent of the stock of Ecuatoriana.

New aircraft were ordered, and the whole airline was given a shake-up. Pride was restored within the airline, and in 2002, the image of 'New Lloyd' was born. New routes were undertaken and further Boeing 727s were ordered. This enabled LAB to have standby aircraft available in the event that the scheduled aircraft for a specific flight became unserviceable. The airline was now 77 years old and had operated an uninterrupted service during this time, making it the second oldest airline in the world behind the Netherlands' KLM.

On 23 December 2002, LAB took delivery of a leased Boeing 767-300ER, registered CP-2425. The aircraft was named *Madrileño*, the name given to a resident of Madrid, and, appropriately, it was used

CP-1698 joined the LAB fleet in June 1981. (Gerry Manning)

on the route to the Spanish capital from Santa Cruz. LAB also followed its competitors in introducing a frequent-flyers club under the brand name of 'Lider' and significantly improved its online systems to produce more detailed and up-to-date flight information for passengers. A second aircraft of the same type joined the fleet in February 2003 and was named *Oriente*, the name given to the first aircraft ever operated by the airline. This aircraft carried the registration CP-2426. Additionally, a further Boeing 727-200 joined the fleet in December 2003. This was a cargo version, registered as CP-2428 and named *Ekeko* – the god of abundance and prosperity according to the people of the Bolivian Altiplano.

With this expansion, by the end of 2002, LAB's staff now numbered more than 1,700, with more than 20,000 people being employed indirectly. The government owned all but a few of the shares. The network consisted of 21 domestic destinations and 15 international ones, all of them in South America, with the exception of Miami. The international routes were served by the Boeing 707s and Boeing 727s, while the domestic routes were operated by a combination of the Boeing 727s and Fairchild F-27s. The airline was carrying about 1.3 million passengers per year. A Boeing 727-200 was also added to the fleet and named *Andean Liberator*. In 2004, LAB began a new route to Washington DC, becoming the only South American airline to operate into the US capital. International routes that had previously been dropped, such as those to the Argentinian cities of Salta and Córdoba, Havana (Cuba), and the Brazilian cities of Manaus and Rio de Janeiro were reintroduced. A further change in 2004 involved a complete change to the LAB colour scheme. Dark blue was chosen to represent stability and reflect the airline's history. Orange was also added to reflect warmth and congeniality. The overall impression

CP-1698 served LAB for almost 20 years before being sold Brazilian airline, Brasair Transportes Aéreos. (Gerry Manning)

Another view of the hard-working CP-1698. (Gerry Manning)

was to present LAB as a modern airline. LAB was one of the earliest airlines to be founded in Latin America, and on 15 September 2000, it marked its 75th anniversary. A number of awards were issued to LAB to commemorate this, by both the municipal and central governments.

Although the airline was running a full schedule, it still was not making money. LAB had not presented a balance sheet since 2003 and had huge debts, which meant it stopped paying salaries and pension contributions. In early 2006, LAB pilots went on strike, leading to widespread conflict, from which the government of the newly inaugurated President Evo Morales tried to distance himself. Asbún, like many traditional aeronautical entrepreneurs, thought the government should pay for his shortcomings, and the workers, who despite the fact they did not like Asbún, also thought the government should pay to maintain the company. When LAB turned 78 in 2003, the company published a booklet with a photo of Tito Asbún on the cover.

On 8 August 2006, a new idea was put forward to LAB. A British-based consortium called Trans-Atlantic Airways (TAA) approached the airline with a view to investing in it. The company's plan was to take over administration of the LAB for a five-year term and buy the Asbún shares in exchange for injecting significant capital. There was much enthusiasm for the idea, and Asbún, with the approval of the LAB staff, transferred the shares to TAA, which now became the majority shareholder. This had the effect of the employees withdrawing their numerous outstanding lawsuits against Asbún.

However, matters did not go to plan. Just seven days later, TAA suddenly announced they were no longer interested in taking over LAB's debts. Investigations were made into TAA, revealing that the company was not registered in Britain and its declared address was in fact a restaurant. The LAB staff then tried to recover the shares that TAA had agreed to return to Asbún. Finally, the funds were

This aircraft was converted to an all-cargo configuration during its time with LAB. (Gerry Manning)

reimbursed to the Trade Union Federation of LAB staff. Complaints of fraud were filed against TAA officials, but little more was heard of it. By now, the LAB employees were the only ones interested in keeping the company in business, albeit on a much smaller scale than previously.

It was evident the airline would hardly return to full business, fundamentally because the government no longer had any interest in supporting it. This encouraged AeroSur to increase its activity. In August 2006, it had begun flying to Miami using a leased Boeing 757 and it signed a codeshare agreement with TACA, an El Salvador-based airline primarily serving Central America. By April 2007, AeroSur was controlling about 90 per cent of the Bolivian market. At the same time, Austral, an Argentine airline, and LAN-Peru requested permission to operate to Bolivia, thus putting them in direct competition with LAB.

In 2006, LAB's revenue began to decline once more. Remedial action meant that its network had to be reduced and during that year many routes, especially the international ones, were cancelled. This meant the airline could no longer afford the leases on its long-haul aircraft, which were a mixture of Airbus A310s, Boeing 757s, 767s and Lockheed L-1011s. This was clearly a very mixed fleet, with little commonality in spares holding, crew resources and ground equipment, which in any airline causes many maintenance and operational problems and is, therefore, costly. The only redeeming feature was that the aircraft were leased and thus could be returned quickly to the lessors.

Because of an additional debt of US$1.6 million, largely the result of missed lease payments, LAB also lost the possibility to sell tickets on international traffic routes, through fear the aircraft would be impounded. The fleet was reduced to just six Boeing 727s in 2006 because customs seized another aircraft, which had arrived the previous year, but its entry into the country 'was never legalized, despite repeated requests made to the company,' said Eduardo Navarro, Director of Customs. In February

This is the most photographed of the LAB Boeing 707s, perhaps because it did the most work. (Bob O'Brien Collection)

2007, the government had intervened to help, but a month later, the Constitutional Court had allowed an appeal filed by the company. This led the LAB staff to demand the resignation of the principal shareholder, Ernesto Asbún, who had bought 50 per cent of the shares sold by VASP when the airline was privatised. He and media mogul Raúl Garáfulic, after taking over the management of LAB, failed to pay any social security contributions or government taxes, thus increasing the debt of the airline even more. There were no explanations made or professional audits undertaken during this time. Staff claimed not to have been paid, and the employees demanded the government take action. This was supported by a number of other organisations in Cochabamba and led to violent demonstrations, with the seizure of the headquarters of the Federación de Empresarios Privados union and a threat to set fire to the home of Asbún.

Following the debacle with TAA, it was clear that investment was still needed. The problem was that it was unclear who now owned the company – the first question a potential investor would ask. Although the shares were now in the hands of the employees, they were not registered as such, so legally the company was not official. The only way out of this conundrum was either for the government to take the airline over again, or liquidation. It quickly became apparent that Bolivia's president, Evo Morales, was not in favour of a takeover. His judgement was no doubt based on the fact that no salaries had been paid for ten months and the creditors were snapping up the few assets that remained. Only one aircraft in the fleet was airworthy, which made irregular internal flights. As if all this were not enough, the employees had elected Franklin Taendler, a Bolivian businessman, as CEO of the airline; however, he was later arrested following complaints from the very employees who had voted for him, accused of misdemeanours within the airline, for example paying exorbitant executive salaries and having devious dealings with travel agents. This included the lease of an L-1011 TriStar and offering charter flights to Madrid, which were not economical for the airline. The TriStar was a type that, by common consent, was unviable for LAB's operation.

In mid-2007, an American company called Swiss Transatlantic entered into the picture, offering to purchase the employees' shares for about US$80 million. It is not known whether it was related in any way to the original British-based suitors. Swiss Transatlantic requested the revocation of the of the suspended operating licence as a condition of the purchase. The authorities said it could only be done if the company could demonstrate that its aircraft were airworthy, that the crews' licences were current, and that full insurance coverage was in place. Curiously, considering the amount of money involved and the potential complications, all the negotiations took place by phone, thus leaving an air of uncertainty over the deal. Swiss Transatlantic later proposed a joint venture, in which it would inject an initial operating capital of US$6m, plus its own administration. This time they did visit the airline, but no deal was reached, and negotiations continued. A month later, a joint-venture agreement was signed, but the details were not disclosed to the media. In August, the LAB shareholders approved the transfer of shares to Swiss Transatlantic, which quickly appointed a new board of directors while announcing that the flights to the US would begin again.

As a result of the deal. the Bolivian treasury immediately claimed its debts, including seizing LAB assets. As a result, Swiss Transatlantic decided to withdraw, citing 'lack of guarantees and legal certainty'. Its delegates returned to Bolivia for further discussions; they ratified the contract and then left. Because LAB had not flown for some months, it would have had to make a flight before 20 November to keep its air operator's certificate valid. One aircraft, a Boeing 727-200, had been kept in an airworthy condition, thanks to parts provided by a Peruvian airline. When they checked all the

Despite the fact that its Boeing 707s were operated in a combi configuration, all the windows were left intact. (Bob O'Brien Collection)

documentation, they realised that the aircraft's insurance had expired, and they had no funds with which to pay for the premium. The DGCA granted an extension until 25 December. The significance of the date was not lost on Swiss Transatlantic, which, to everyone's surprise, reappeared and paid the insurance. On 23 December, LAB flew once more, on a charter flight routing Cochabamba–Santa Cruz–Cochabamba. The flight had been chartered by four travel agencies, since there was no government agreement to sell tickets or carry out regular flights, so the only possibility was a third-party charter. The operation came as a shock to both the main Bolivian airlines – Aerolíneas Sudamericanas and AeroSur – which saw the potential new operation as a threat and immediately went to court to have any future operations blocked. Aerolíneas Sudamericanas also allegedly tried to extort the travel agents who worked closely with LAB.

The charter flight had raised the optimism of the LAB employees, although there was little revenue to back up the optimism. There was talk of operating three aircraft, the previous VASP colour scheme was replaced and the aircraft were being made airworthy. However, LAB's relationship with the regulatory authorities was less than cordial, and the process of bringing the aircraft up to airworthiness standard became very protracted. An aircraft did operate on 1 January 2008, but it crashed on approach to Trinidad while operating a charter for TAM. The details are recorded in the fleet list, but the fact that the aircraft ran out of fuel may have been indicative of LAB's financial difficulties.

That was LAB's last flight. There were aircraft still on LAB's books, but they had not been well looked-after and, in fact, had also accumulated debts on missed lease payments. Once more, Swiss Transatlantic appeared on the scene, offering to reinvest in the airline, but only on the condition that its five directors were reinstated. In April 2008, another aircraft was made airworthy, but in an ironic twist of fate it was leased to LAB's two competitors.

The large cargo door is clearly visible on this image of CP-1365. (Bob O'Brien Collection)

The early turbofan Pratt & Whitney JT-3D engines were fitted to LAB's Boeing 707s. (Bob O'Brien Collection)

On 30 March 2007, the Bolivian government took the very difficult decision to close down the airline, and within 48 hours all flights were suspended. The aircraft on lease were returned to the lessors and those owned by LAB were parked at Cochabamba. To stop the constant flow of supportive money, the government's decision to close down the airline had been rapid, and given LAB's extensive network, this left the country almost without any flights, and it was not until October 2007 that a new airline began operating with government approval. Boliviana de Aviación was established, to become the new Bolivian flag carrier that same month. Following this, LAB was allowed to operate a number of charter flights for AeroSur during late 2007 and early 2008. This meant that, from 1 April 2007, the airline had ceased to exist. LAB, the second oldest airline in South America behind Avianca, would be forced to suspend its operations because it had become overwhelmed by debts and could not even purchase fuel. The financial manager, Carlos de Marchi, had said that revenues had fallen to the point where even reducing the number of flights would not solve the problem. LAB had no option but to reduce its flights after returning two of its leased aircraft, a Boeing 757, registered N958PG, in September 2005 and a Boeing 727-200, CP-2427, to the US leasing company Pegasus, to which the airline owed an accumulated debt of US$7 million.

To explain one of the reasons for the crisis, the transport minister, Wilson Villarroel, cited the example of Aerolíneas Argentinas, which with 1,200 employees operated a fleet of 55 aircraft; whereas LAB, with only six aircraft, had 2,035 employees. The staff began to post strike pickets at several areas aournd the headquarters in Cochabamba, 311 miles (500km) southeast of La Paz. The staff wanted the government to nationalise the company again. It had previously been nationalised to prevent its collapse, but President Morales refused to do so again, saying it would be absurd to nationalise a US$160 million debt that had been taken over by a corrupt administration. The financial crisis had come to light in January after the pilots demanded the payment of outstanding salaries, and it was revealed the company had failed to deposit US$3.6m into the employee pension fund.

In April 2010, the Bolivian Company Supervision and Social Control Authority stated that LAB should be liquidated because it had lost 87 per cent of its capital. No sooner had this announcement been made when a company called Wolfram Mannebach, based in Luxembourg, made an offer for the workers' shares, but as with so many of these initiatives, it came to nothing.

It now became apparent to all concerned that the shares owned by the employees were not worth the paper they were written on. There were a number of shareholders' meetings, and the authorities set out steps that they wanted the company to follow. The shares were the basis of the pension fund, and since they had virtually no value, there was an allegation of fraud against the shareholders. The authorities believed that LAB owed more than 600 million bolivars in taxes, wages, lawsuits and lost wages.

A shareholders' meeting was held on 15 May, but it was inconclusive. There was no solution to the liquidation problem and no reduction in the capital holding. There were a number of objections raised at the meeting and, once again, the legal brains were brought into the argument. This time,

LAB operated four A310s on a lease basis. This aircraft was initially registered as CP-2338. (Gerry Manning)

Another view of CP-2232 arriving at Cochabamba in 1992. (Gerry Manning)

the charges were against managers for breach of duties and general mismanagement. As a form of compensation, LAB offered the government three aircraft: an airworthy Boeing 727-200; a -100 series, which was not airworthy; and a Boeing 737-300 (CP-2313), which had been leased to an Indonesian company called Lorena Air since 2008, but its condition was unknown. Undeterred by this, the shareholders offered it as a potential presidential aircraft. Of these, only the 727-200 was accepted on a lease agreement by TAM.

One more attempt to save the company was made in October 2010, when the shareholders met once more. This time, they suggested forming LAB into a maintenance and leasing company. Third-party maintenance was still being carried out at this time, and LAB had a fully equipped hangar. It had aircraft, but, by this time, none of them were in an airworthy condition. The shareholders believed that since the Swiss Transatlantic funding offer made in 2007 had never been withdrawn, the offer was still on the table, and they set about trying to recover this money.

AeroSur was a privately owned airline, founded in August 1992 and based in Santa Cruz. It had been established following the deregulation of Bolivia's airline industry in 1992 and had built up a significant route network, becoming a major competitor of LAB. When LAB went bankrupt in

Turnaround time at Cochabamba for CP-2232. (Gerry Manning)

2007, AeroSur became Bolivia's largest airline. Its mixed fleet consisted of aircraft ranging from 19-seat Swearingen Metros to Boeing 767s, and it operated a network of domestic and international scheduled services. However, on 12 March 2012, it suspended operations because of unpaid taxes. Services resumed again on 6 April, although the Madrid route was discontinued. AeroSur eventually followed LAB into bankruptcy and finally suspended operations on 17 May 2012. Despite an attempt by a US investor, William Petty, who had mining interests in Bolivia and had signed a memorandum of understanding with the intention of investing up to US$15m into the ailing carrier, the negotiations came to nothing, and AeroSur's air operator's certificate was formally withdrawn in July 2012.

Having lost LAB, the government was keen to establish another flag carrier. It had prepared a plan to guarantee air transport in the country, given the imminent bankruptcy of LAB. The Directorate of Civil Aeronautics decreed that the routes would be covered by three independent airlines. Boliviana de Aviación had been set up in 2007 during the government of Evo Morales. All the funding was made available by the government, and with two Boeing 737-200s it began operating the main domestic routes to La Paz, Salida and Santa Cruz from its base in Cochabamba.

Amaszonas, an airline based in La Paz and operating Bombardier CRJ-200s, operated both scheduled and charter flights, generally in the north of the country. Amaszonas had been founded in 2000. The third company, Aerocon, a regional carrier with a small fleet of turbo-prop aircraft, was based in the Beni region of Trinidad. After failing to meet operational deadlines set by the Directorate of Civil Aeronautics following the write-off of two of their Swearingen Metroliners within four months during 2013, the company forfeited its operating licence in June 2015.

Another view of CP-2426 in the maintenance area at Cochabamba. (Michael Prophet)

The LAB maintenance base forms the background as Boeing 767-300ER CP-2426 receives attention. (Michael Prophet)

Britannia Airways G-BLKV showing its hybrid scheme at Miami, during a short lease to LAB between November 1989 and January 1990. (aussieairliners.com)

Addendum

There can no doubt that, from its inception, LAB fulfilled a very important role in developing air transport in Bolivia, often against considerable odds. The most import function it provided initially was connecting the highlands and the valleys with the east in what, by any standards, were challenging circumstances. Later, it connected the central axes – La Paz Cochabamba and Santa Cruz – with the north and south of the country.

Particularly important, and certainly more challenging, was the opening up of routes into small towns, which did not have access by road or railway. There have been references elsewhere to the lack of a structured rail network in Bolivia, and it is deserving of greater examination, given the role it played, albeit unintentionally, in promoting domestic air travel in the country. The history of the railway network is peculiar. This was due to a number of factors, some of which were beyond the control of the government, and not least of which was the loss of the direct line to the Bolivian coast following the 1879–83 War of the Pacific. The loss of Bolivia's only port meant there was no incentive to build what arguably would have been the most important line within Bolivian territory. As a result of this setback, the concept of rail travel came much later to Bolivia than to other countries in South America.

It is not generally known, but the British contributed much to the early development of the railways in South America. The railways built in Peru followed the standard 4ft 8½in gauge (1.435m) set in Britain in the 19th century. The rapidly expanding mining sector in Bolivia allowed for a large expansion of railway traffic based on freight-carrying during the 1920s but by-passed the major population centres and their requirements for travel. Following an agreement with Chile after the War of the Pacific, Bolivia was once again allowed to operate a railway system from the mines to the coast. The railways had been built by independent operators, usually from the mining industry which, by nature, was very competitive. Thus, the lines did not join up with each other. Indeed, many of these lines remained uncompleted until the 1950s, by which time Bolivia had a mixture of the British standard gauge and a 3ft 3⅜in (1m) gauge, which were, naturally, completely incompatible.

The 1953 revolution led to the installation of a left-wing government. One of the first actions of the new regime was to nationalise the railways. A company called Empressa Ferrocarril Nacional de Bolivia (Bolivian National Railway Company) was formed but required substantial investment for it to operate efficiently. Unfortunately, this investment never arrived, meaning the most efficient way of moving around the country continued to be by air. Money was instead invested into improving the road system.

On Lake Titicaca, the railway still runs to the port of Puno on the Peruvian side, where the rolling stock is transferred onto a dual gauge car float, which operates to Guaqui in Bolivia, thus linking the Peruvian gauge with the Bolivian gauge. As if this were not complicated enough, it does not fit well with the lines in other countries. For example, most railways in Argentina have a gauge of 5ft 6in (1.67m), making any sort of overland transfer for locomotives and rolling stock impossible. From this it can be seen that there were two major obstacles to improving rail transport within the boundaries of Bolivia, and this is one of the reasons why domestic air travel became so important. In more recent years, this has changed, with 78 per cent of goods in 2015 carried by rail in the eastern area of the country, and with Bolivia now having access to the Pacific port of Arica in Chile. Though even today, only about 11 per cent of all roads in Bolivia are paved. There are about 855 airfields, many of which are simple strips, often used by farmers. Of these, only 21 have paved runways. For all this, passenger figures are still relatively low, with just 4.1 million passengers carried on scheduled airlines in 2018.

There is little doubt that, from its inception, LAB was given a considerable amount of state assistance during its existence. Some of this was overt, in the form of straightforward grants after the government initially invested 150,000 bolivars in LAB shares and then a further 200,000 bolivars in 1932. The government also provided significant financial assistance to the airline during the Gran Chaco War. Other benefits were less obvious, taking the form of fuel subsides and the installation of airport equipment. There can also be little doubt that at other times, when LAB found itself in financial difficulties, the government injected funds into the airline, for example with route subsidies. In May 1946, the Central Bank provided a loan of US$350,000 for improved technical and administrative systems, and in the 1950s a loan of 20 million bolivars was awarded, followed by a loan of 1.2 million bolivars with which to purchase fuel and spare parts. It is not known whether any, or all, of these loans were ever repaid.

Equally, it must be said that this was an airline with a large domestic network, paid for in the local currency, in a country where wage levels were some of the lowest in South America, and where there were few alternatives to flying. As a result of this, the fares would be subsidised by the government, which created an artificial balance sheet.

The former staff of LAB have never fully accepted that the airline went bankrupt and have fought a constant battle in trying to revive the airline. The LAB Workers' Federation, now the de facto owners of the airline, with the resources of $3 million from a local investor, have applied to the General Directorate of Civil Aeronautics (DGAC) to restart operations. The staff also believe that the principal 27 airports in Bolivia still belong to LAB and that this fact can be used as collateral. They also claim to have three aircraft available, one of which is CP-1366, a Boeing 737-200, which has been regularly maintained since LAB's demise.

A Boeing 767 flight simulator still sits in the box in which it was delivered in 2007. In 2021, it was announced that a group of investors from the Abu Dhabi Foundation had expressed an interest in reactivating the airline. The foundation had said that it would invest US$150m to put the airline back in the air again. Both the Telecommunications and Transportation Authority and the DGAC have declared that they have not received a formal request to re-activate the airline. One of the obstacles to restarting the airline is the debt currently owed to the pension fund administration, together with outstanding taxes and workers' salaries. The government has stated that unless these conditions are met, the airline cannot be relaunched.

Acknowledgement is made to the following sources

Contreras, Manuel E, 'Lloyd Aéreo Boliviano (LAB): Pionero de la aviación comercial en América Latina, 1925–1964', *Un siglo de aviación comercial en América Latina (1919–2019)*, eds Javier Vidal and Melina Piglia, Editorial of the University of Magdalena, Santa Marta.

Davies, R. E. G., *Airlines of Latin America since 1919*, Smithsonian Press, 1984

Airline timetable images: http://www.timetableimages.com/ttimages/complete/complete.htm

Friends of Lloyd Aéreo Boliviano: http://www.lloydaereobolivianofriends.com

Lloyd Aéreo Boliviano: http://labairlines.com.bo

LAB fleet list

From the list (below) of all the known aircraft operated by LAB, it quickly becomes apparent that the accident rate is significant. However, from the introduction, it can be seen that this is no ordinary country with simple hills and valleys. It is also subject to extreme weather events, which certainly in the early days of aviation were not able to be accurately predicted by weather forecasters. It was the intervention of Panagra in the 1960s that set up a more accurate forecasting system, but even in developed countries with more stable climates, weather forecasting in the 1960s was nowhere near as accurate as it is today. The conditions around the Andes often brought about unexpected turbulence, and electrical storms could interfere with radios and navigational equipment. So, unfortunate as it may have been, it is not entirely surprising that so many accidents occurred; the statistics should be read with that in mind. A further point concerns the airfields themselves, particularly those in the Beni region. Many of these were little more than prepared strips. Many would have no air traffic control facilities and only the most rudimentary shelter for passengers. The airfields would be unfenced and animals would graze the area, often having to be scared off by a low pass or two.

What is also clear is that, in many cases, there is little or no explanation for the cause of the accident. Usually, the crew would lose their lives; often, the accident could be in a quite remote area and no one would see it. As onboard radios became available after the arrival of the DC-3s and C-46, and air traffic control systems were set up at the busier airports, some of the dangers were reduced. The mountains obstructed radio transmissions, however, and any mayday calls put out by the aircraft would not necessarily have been heard. There was no dedicated procedure for investigating accidents, and any investigations that did exist would be undertaken by the police or the army, neither of which had experience of, or training for, dealing with such events and could only operate within their own rules. They were not tasked with investigating the causes of the accidents, rather dealing with the results of them. Despite its somewhat dubious accident record, LAB was the first airline, apart from Alitalia, to fly The Pope, an achievement the airline is justifiably very proud of.

For reference, the acronyms used in the table below are as follows:

ASN   Aviation Safety Network

CFIT   Controlled flight into terrain. In other words, the aircraft was under the control of the crew when it crashed. Terrain in this case refers to the surface features of an area of land

ntu   not taken up

w/o   written off

wfu   withdrawn from use

LAB fleet, 1925–2007

Date	Identity	C/N	Fate
JUNKERS F 13			
27 Jul 1925	El Oriente	0769	w/o 6 Nov 1926
Jan 1926	Beni	0711	w/o 26 Jan 1926
31 Dec 1926	Oriente	0710	w/o 29 Aug 1929?
1925	Beni II		
1926	Beni III	788	
1926	Chargas		Transferred to FAB in 1933
1927	Oriente II		w/o 26 Aug 1929
16 Apr 1928	Chaco		w/o 5 Jul 1928
16 Apr 1928	Mamoré	0634	Floatplane. Ex-Lloyd Aéreo Córdoba. Sold in US 1942
16 Apr 1928	Illimani		w/o 1939
Junkers W 33/34			
1933	CB-19 Mururata	2756	w/o Apr 1939
1933	CB-20 Sajama		w/o 13 March 1937 near Cuibaja
1929	Tunari	2608	In service 1929–42
1929	Vanguardia	2607	w/o 12 Apr 1939 at Villavicencio
Ford TriMotor 5-AT			
Mar 1932	Cruz del Sur	100	Crashed after take-off from Villamontes in the Gran Chaco region on 26 October 1932. It had been delivering wartime supplies to the Bolivian Army.
Junkers Ju 52/3m			
May 1932	CB-17 Juan del Valle	4008	First production aircraft. Crashed on 3 Nov 1940 at Rincón del Tigre, Chiquitos. The wreckage was not discovered until January 1942.
1932	CB-18 Huanuni	4009	Second production aircraft. Crashed and w/o 15 December 1937 at Sorata en route La Paz–Apolo.
1932	CB-21 Bolivar	4061	Sold to Argentina in 1943.
1932	CB-22 Illampu	5623	In service 1932–44. Sold to VASP Brazil.
1932	CB-32 Chorolque	4018	Crashed in the Tapacarí swamps, northeast of Cochabamba on 17 January 1936.

Date	Identity	C/N	Fate
Sikorsky S-38B			
1933	*El Marihúi*	414-11	Ex-NC20V crashed in Cochabamba on 27 September 1935 en route from Trinidad to Todos Santos. The crew attempted an emergency landing on water at Aguas Negras but came to rest in a muddy field. The pilots were later able to leave, but the weather had deteriorated, and the aircraft hit a mountain slope and was wrecked. Both pilots were injured.
1933	*Nicolás Suárez*	414-15	Crashed in Guayaramerín on 10 October 1941. Originally owned by Howard Hughes as NC24V.
Junkers -A 50 Junior			
1933	*Acre*		
1933	*Piray*		
1933	*Warnes*		
This was a two-seater low-wing monoplane, presumably used for training, but no further details are known. Only 50 were ever built.			
Junkers Ju 86			
1937	CB-23 *Illimani*	860013	Civil passenger version.
1937	*Mariscal Santa Cruz*	K-7 Variant 860234	
1937	*General Perez*	K-7 Variant 860237	
1937	*Mariscal Sucre*	K-7 Variant 860240	Ex-Lloyd Aéreo Córdoba.
Grumman G-21A Goose			
Jul 1938	CB-24 *Moxos*	1015	ntu
Junkers W 34 (Trainer)			
1933	CB-19 *Mururata*	2576	Crashed on 3 April 1939.
1933	CB-20 *Sajama*		Crashed en route to La Paz at Cuybaja on 13 March 1937.
Lockheed 18 Lodestar			
1941	CB-25	18-2088	Destroyed by fire at El Alto, 21 August 1944.

Date	Identity	C/N	Fate
1942	CB-26	18-2098	w/o 6 Sep 1949 at Sucre. Crashed after being hit by government anti-aircraft fire while on a supporting flight for rebels during a civil war.
4 Mar 1943	CB-27	18-2169	Believed to have been broken up for spares.
8 Dec 1944	CB-28	18-2217	Believed to have been the target of an air attack on 29 August 1949 in Sucre during a revolution. One engine caught fire and the aircraft was destroyed.
Douglas DC-3 and derivatives			
Aug 1945	CB-29 C-53C-DO Skytrooper	4980	The Skytrooper was a basic version of the C-47 with military-style seating. Re-registered as CP-529. Damaged while on lease to Sudamericana. Later destroyed by fire during an engine run after being sold to Frigorifico Santa Rita.
Aug 1945	CB-30 C-47B-DK	34351	Re-registered as CP-530 on 1 Oct 1953. In service until September 1961.
Aug 1945	CB-31 C-47A-DL	13837	w/o 1 Jan 1951 at La Paz. Circumstances unknown.
1945	CB-32 C-47A-75-DL	19445	w/o 29 May 1947 after crashing in a swamp near Mamoré.
1945	CB-33 C-47	20080	w/o 28 Aug 1949 at Cochabamba. During the revolution, the government sent aircraft with troops to quell the situation. Some of the fighting took place around the airport at Cochabamba, and fuel tanks, hangars and planes were attacked. The fighting took place over two days and extended throughout the city.
20 Aug 1945	CB-34 C-47A-10DK	12570	Ex-Panagra. Damaged 15 April 1953 near Pilcomayo. Re-registered as CP-534 but ntu. Re-registered as CP-607 June 1954 and later transferred to YPFB.
Aug 1945	CB-35 C-53 DO Skytrooper	4867	Ex-Panagra. Re-registered as CP-535 on 1 October 1957. Crashed into a mountain near Savari while on a scheduled flight from Cochabamba to Oruro on 18 March 1957. CFIT.
15 Apr 1948	CB-36 C-47B-DL	20619	Re-registered as CP-536. Crashed and w/o near Cochabamba during a test flight following a 6-monthly maintenance check on 21 August 1962.
1947	CB-68 C-47A-65-DL	19024	Re-registered as CP-568 10 Jan 1953. Crashed 4 Feb 1964 shortly after t/o near Yacuiba airport and w/o.
Jan 1951	CB-72 C-49E-DO	1549	Originally adapted as a sleeper aircraft for American Airlines. Re-registered on 10 Jan 1953 as CP-572. Involved in a mid-air collision with an LAB B-17 (CP-597), while flying in the Beni region on 5 September 1955. The B-17 crashed and was w/o, but the DC-3 landed safely at Trinidad, and after extensive repairs was later returned to service.

LAB fleet list

Date	Identity	C/N	Fate
1951	CB-73 C-47-DL	4682	Re-registered as CP-573. In service until 1975.
22 Jul 1951	CB-83 C-47A-35-DL	9668	Re-registered as CP-583 in October 1953. Later sold within Bolivia and seized in 1990 for drug-running in Trinidad, Bolivia.
Aug 1951	CB-84 Douglas C-47A-DL	19226	Re-registered as CP-584 on 1 January 1953. Crashed and w/o 31 December 1959 shortly after taking off from San José de Chiquitos Airport.
Sep 1951	CB-91 Douglas C-47A-90-DL	20200	Re-registered as CP-591 on 1 October 1953. In service September 1951–75. Wfu Cochabamba and used for parts.
Jun 1953	CB-100 Douglas DC-3-214	2181	Re-registered as CP-600 in October 1953. Crashed near Tarabuco on the top of the Rodeo Pampa mountain range, some 38 miles (60km) southeast of Sucre en route to Sucre from Camiri on 3 November 1953. CFIT.
Jun 1953	CB-101 Douglas DC-3-214	2182	Re-registered as CP-601 in October 1953. Suffered a tyre blow-out at Potosí on 15 January 1964. Eventually repaired and then re-registered as CP 733. Returned to service in November 1964. Sold on by 1970.
Apr 1954	CP-605 Douglas C-47B-28-DK	32542	Crashed on approach to La Paz on 25 August 1956 following the loss of a propeller while on a cargo flight and subsequently w/o.
Jun 1963	CP-733 see CB-101		
Jun 1965	CP-734 Douglas C-47B-DK	34312	w/o 19 April 1968 at Trinidad following an engine failure on take-off. The aircraft was operating a scheduled flight from Trinidad to La Paz.
27 Mar 1965	CP-735 Douglas C-47B-DK	33553	Sold to Vibas Bolivia in 1975. The aircraft crashed into a mountain at an altitude of 17,815ft (5,430m) on 19 Oct 1999, while carrying beef from Yacuma and heading for La Paz. The wreckage was only found six years later. The body of the co-pilot was not located until November 2010.
Curtiss C-46 Commando			
10 Aug 1949	CB-37 C46A-60-K	433	w/o Rurrenabaque, Bolivia – details unknown.
17 Jan 1950	CB-50 CA-1-CU	26397	Sold to Loide Aero Nacional of Brazil on 24 July 1951.
11 Feb 1950	CB-51 C-46A	26369	w/o Cochabamba on 24 Apr 1950 – details unknown.
1950	CB-38 C-46A		w/o at Laguna Anteojos o Azar on 2 October 1950 – details unknown.

Date	Identity	C/N	Fate
4 Dec 1949	CP-539 C-46A	26488	Damaged in Cochabamba on 24 April 1950, then repaired and w/o 29 July 1951 during take-off from Cochabamba on a delivery flight to Brazil. The aircraft had been bought eight days previously by Loide Aéreo Nacional of Brazil. During the take-off from Cochabamba, while in the initial climb, the aircraft hit a tree. The aircraft was apparently still registered as CB-39. CP-539 was never taken up.
Aug 1963	CP-730 C-46D-CU	33457	Leased from Aerovias Condor. Crashed and w/o San Benito, Bolivia on 3 August 1966 while on a cargo flight from Riberalta to Cochabamba. The aircraft disappeared. The wreckage was not found until 12 days later. Believed CFIT.
Douglas DC-4A			
1954	CP-609	10510	w/o 5 February 1960. Engine caught fire and aircraft crashed shortly after take-off 15km south of Laguna Huañacota following an engine fire. The aircraft was on a scheduled passenger flight from Cochabamba to La Paz.
Mar 1955	CP-610	10538	On 26 September 1956, the first hijacking of a commercial flight for political purposes was that of an LAB flight. The aircraft was carrying 47 prisoners. They were being transported from Santa Cruz to La Paz. There they were to be taken to a concentration camp located in the town of Oruro. Two of the prisoners gained control of the aircraft in mid-flight and re-routed the plane to Tartagal, Argentina. However, air traffic control gave instructions to re-route to Salta Argentina, as the airfield in Tartagal was not big enough for the DC-4. They did as they were instructed and later arrived safely in the city of Salta. The prisoners told the Argentinian government of the injustices they had been subjected to and received political asylum. To US 1961.
1960	CP-682	27249	Left service in 1962. To UK and converted to ATL-98 Carvair c/n 9 as G-ASHZ.
Douglas DC-6B			
15 Dec 1960	CP-698	43273	w/o 26 September 1969. The aircraft flew into the side of Mount Choquetanga en route from Santa Cruz to La Paz. The flight was carrying 16 members of one of Bolivia's top football teams. The wreckage was not found until three days later.
9 Nov 1961	CP-707	43547	w/o 15 March 1963 on Chachakumani Peak, Bolivia. CFIT. The aircraft was en route between Arica (Chile) and La Paz.

Date	Identity	C/N	Fate
24 Jul 1963	CP-715	43543	In service 1963–74. To FAB.
Jan 1964	CP-740	43272	To Air Beni and registered as CP-2291, but later burnt while on the ground. Some repair work had been done on the aircraft, and a mechanic and a flight engineer went on board to start the engines. Suddenly, a fire erupted in the number 2 engine, and both crewmembers fled from the aircraft without following the correct emergency procedures. It is thought the fuel pumps were operating at high pressure. The fire spread, destroying part of the fuselage. The airport firefighting services were practising elsewhere on the airport and failed to reach the scene in time to put out the fire, and the aircraft was destroyed. A local newspaper suggested that the aircraft might have been set on fire deliberately, because a plastic bottle was found in the number 2 engine, containing a fuel, apparently kerosene, different from the fuel normally used by the DC-6B. The aircraft had been insured for US$360,000. (Acknowledgements ASN).
Boeing B-17			
1951	CB-70 B-17F	8296	Re-registered CP-570 1953. Crashed and w/o 21 September 1955 at La Paz airport. Circumstances unknown.
1950	CB-71 B-17F	6035	Re-registered CP-571. Subleased to Aerolíneas Moxos and w/o at Viacha on 16 January 1962.
5 Aug 1951	CB-79 B-17F	3119	Re-reg as CP-579. Crashed near Uncía on 29 December 1958 while being operated by Frigorificos Grigota on lease from LAB. Circumstances unknown.
Nov 1956	CP-620 B-17G	8749	Fitted with cargo door. In service until 1968. Sold to the US and one of five Aircraft Specialties B-17s flown to Hawaii in January 1969 for the movie *Tora! Tora! Tora!*
Dec 1956	CP-621 B-17G	8683	Originally delivered to the FAB on 22 June 1956. Fitted with cargo door. In service until September 1968. Sold to the US and one of five Aircraft Specialties B-17s flown to Hawaii in January 1969 for the movie *Tora! Tora! Tora!*
Nov 1956	CP-623 B-17G	32391	Originally delivered to the FAB in 1956. Believed to have been destroyed on 28 July 1958 at La Paz.

Date	Identity	C/N	Fate
Nov 1956	CP-625 B-17G	10285	Believed to have been w/o in an accident at San Lorenzo on 17 Nov 1959.
Jan 1957	CP-627 B-17G	22616	Fitted with large freight door. Undercarriage problem caused belly landing at La Paz on 27 August 1968. The aircraft was rebuilt using parts recovered from CP-580. It was then re-registered as CP-891 in 1969 and subsequently sold to Frigorifico Reyes in La Paz in 1975.
No date	CP-633 Boeing B-17-65-DL	8406	There is some confusion about this registration. In fact, the aircraft never belonged to LAB, nor did it ever carry the registration. The aircraft held the tail number N9815F and was fully repainted in Miami in 1959, but although the registration was issued, the aircraft never used it. There is an image showing a colour scheme with the letters 'LAB'. This is not Lloyd Aéreo Boliviano, but Linea Aérea Borinquen, a Nicaraguan company. The company went out of business in 1960. The registration CP-633 appears to have been allocated, but it was ntu. The aircraft was subsequently sold to Aeropesca Colombia in 1962 as HK-580X (later HK-580) and operated by Aerolíneas del Caribe. It is believed to have crashed in 1962 in Puerto Asis, southern Colombia.
Sep 1960	CP-686 B-17F	6369	Destroyed at Trinidad on 4 November 1965. No further details.
5 Aug 1951	CB-80 Boeing B-17G	9300	Re-registered as CP-580. Believed to have crashed at La Paz on 7 February 1965, but parts used to rebuild CP-627.
Early 1950s	CB-88 B-17G	22555	Re-registered as CP-588. Sold/leased to Aerovias Moxos and w/o at an unknown location on 2 May 1963.
1952	CB-97 B-17G-65-BO	8286	Re-registered as CP-597. On 5 September 1955 it suffered a mid-air collision with LAB DC-3 CP-572 (p. 86), which was on a scheduled passenger flight near Cochabamba. The aircraft crashed near Cochabamba, killing the three crew. The DC-3 was substantially damaged in the collision, but the pilot was able to make an emergency landing at Trinidad airport; no injuries were sustained by the passengers or crew. The DC-3 was repaired and returned to service.

Date	Identity	C/N	Fate
Lockheed L-188 Electra			
12 Aug 1968	CP-853	1125	Ex-American Airlines N6134A. In service 1968–73. Transferred to FAB as TAM-69 until May 1975 and re-registered as TAM-01.
Boeing 707			
Sep 1977	CP-1365 Boeing 707-323C	18692	Aircraft destroyed in a hangar fire on 31 August 1991 in Dothan Alabama. It is believed to have been undergoing a repaint at the time.
Jun 1981	CP-1698 Boeing 707-323C	19586	Sold to Brasair Transportes Aéreos 2000.
Oct 1976	N730JP Boeing 707-131C	17671	Sub-leased from Jet Power USA for a cargo flight. Crashed on take-off from Santa Cruz and w/o 13 October 1976. The aircraft crashed during take-off from El Trompillo Airport, Santa Cruz in Bolivia, killing all three crew members and 88 persons on the ground. A further 78 people were seriously injured. The aircraft was being operated on a round trip from Miami to Santa Cruz. The aircraft had delivered oil-well machinery and other cargo from Houston, Texas to Santa Cruz before its fatal journey, and was departing back to Miami. The take-off run was seen to be longer than usual, and the aircraft crossed the end of Runway 32 at a height of about 20ft (6m). It struck trees, poles and the roofs of houses while rolling to the left and finally struck the ground inverted some 1,837ft (560m) beyond the runway. The aircraft impacted onto a football pitch, bursting into flames. Analysis of the accident was hampered by unserviceable flight recorders. The flight data recorder (FDR) was not in operation at the time of the accident; when the cassette was opened, the entire tape was found to be wound around the receiving reel. The three radio channels of the cockpit voice recorder (CVR) contained some information, but the cockpit area microphone channel was inoperative and the recording did not contain useful information. The subsequent enquiry ruled out structural and engine failure, flight control malfunction and systems failures as possible causes of the accident.

Date	Identity	C/N	Fate
			The engine-pressure ratio (EPR) gauges showed 2.32, corresponding to the setting for a take-off with dry thrust. On the early models of the Boeing 707-100 series aircraft equipped with Pratt & Whitney JT3C engines, demineralised water could be injected into the engines during take-off, to cool them and increase the available thrust. It was found that the water valves were open at the time of impact, but it was not determined with certainty whether the crew attempted to perform a dry take-off but with reserve water, or whether the water was used with EPRs limited to 2.32 with the possibility of increasing the thrust as and when necessary. It was concluded that the crew failed to select enough thrust to achieve the necessary acceleration for take-off and that a significant contributory factor was crew fatigue. (Acknowledgements ASN)
Boeing 727			
17 Feb 1970	CP-861 Boeing 727-1AO	20279	Withdrawn from service March 2007.
Sep 1974	CP-1070 Boeing 727-171C	19860	Withdrawn from service 2001.
March 1975	CP-1223 Boeing 727-078	18795	Withdrawn from service March 2005. Highest number of cycles (79,000+) on a Boeing 727.
8 Oct 1975	CP-1276 Boeing 727-2K3	21082	The first -200 series delivered to LAB. On 23 January 1985, a bomb exploded after a passenger had gone into the forward lavatory and detonated it while the flight was descending during its flight from La Paz. The passenger was killed, but the aircraft was able to make a safe landing at Santa Cruz. The aircraft was repaired and returned to service but was withdrawn in 2007 and stored at Cochabamba. It carries the bible reference *Ezequiel 36:36* on the side and has been regularly maintained by LAB staff.
17 Mar 1977	CP-1339 Boeing 727-17	20512	Leased from Boeing. Returned 11 August 1978.
4 Aug 1978	CP-1366 Boeing 727-2K3	21494	Leased to AeroSur between July and December 2009. Painted in retro livery and returned to service. Stored.
25 Oct 1978	CP-1367 Boeing 727-2K3	21495	Winglets added by 2004. Withdrawn from service 30 March 2007.

Date	Identity	C/N	Fate
May 2003	CP-2428 Boeing 727-2M7	21502	Leased from Pegasus Leasing US. Returned March 2006. Named *Ekeko*.
Nov 2004	CP-2455 Boeing 727-290	21510	Withdrawn from service 30 March 2007.
Aug 1997	CP-2324 Boeing 727-2M7	21823	Leased from Pegasus Leasing US. Named *Virgen de Urkupina*.
Feb 1996	CP-2294 Boeing 727-2J4F	22079	Operated on a short-term lease from TABA of Brazil. Named *City of Potosí*.
Oct 2003	CP-2427 Boeing 727-2B7	22164	Leased from Pegasus Leasing US. Returned August 2005.
5 Jan 2007	CP-2463 Boeing 727-223	22463	Leased from Aviation Capital Group. To AeroSur.
5 Jan 2007	CP-2464 Boeing 727-223	22464	Leased from Aviation Capital Group. To AeroSur.
11 Dec 2002	CP-2429 Boeing 727-259	22475	The aircraft departed from La Paz on a domestic flight to Cobija on 1 February 2008. The weather at Cobija was unsuitable for a landing, so the aircraft diverted to Trinidad. It appears that by this time the aircraft was short of fuel and had to carry out a forced landing in a jungle clearing 2.6 miles (4km) short of the runway at Trinidad. The fuselage still sits where it crash-landed.
Jun 1997	CP-2323 727-287	22605	The left main landing gear collapsed as the aircraft was taxiing out at Buenos Aires' Ezeiza Airport for a scheduled flight to Santa Cruz on 9 January 2001. An investigation discovered there was corrosion in this area. The aircraft was written off.
Oct 2004	CP-2455 727-287	22606	Leased from Pegasus Leasing US. Withdrawn from use on 30 March 2007.
1982	CP-1741 Boeing 727-2K3	22770	The Boeing customer ID shows it as originally having been ordered by LAB, but the registration was not taken up and the aircraft became N776AL of US Air in 1983.
Fairchild F-27			
6 Oct 1969	CP-862 F-27M	127	On 16 December 1971, during a flight from Sucre to La Paz, a hijacker demanded to be taken to Chile. The aircraft was eventually stormed, and the hijacker arrested. It crashed on 16 March 1984 near Cerro Pilon, on a scheduled flight from Trinidad to San Borja. CFIT.

Date	Identity	C/N	Fate
Jul 1969	CP -863 F-27M	128	Withdrawn from service in 1983. Sold to the US.
1977	CP -1116 F-27J	111	Damaged beyond repair at Cochabamba on 20 December 1984. No other details.
1977	CP-1117 F-27J	118	Crashed into a hillside at Yacuiba on 2 June 1980 while on approach from Cochabamba. CFIT
17 Dec 1974	CP-1175 F-27J	121	While taxiing at Yacuma Airport on 22 January 1980, the aircraft ran off the taxiway and into a ditch. The nosewheel section and propeller were damaged, which then damaged the wing and fuel tanks. This, in turn, started a fire. The aircraft was written off.
1973	CP-1176 F-27J	119	In service until 1988. Sold to Airlift International in the US.
1985	F-GBRU F-27J	43	Leased from Transport Aérien Transrégional of France 1985–87.
Jan 1985	F-GBRV F-27J	44	Leased from Transport Aérien Transrégional of France, 1985–August 1987.
Lockheed L-1011 Tristar			
2006	OD-MIR L-1011-500	1246	Wet leased from Globe Jet Airlines.
2006	OD-ZEE L-1011-500	1239	Wet leased from Globe Jet Airlines.
Airbus A300			
1990	PP-SNN A300B4-203	225	Leased from VASP, 1990–91.
Airbus A310			
1995	CP-2273 A310-304	475	Leased from GECAS, 1995–97.
1996	CP-2307 A310-204	661	Leased from ILFC, 1996–99.
Nov 1991	CP-2338 A310-304	562	Leased 1991–2004. Re-registered as CP-2332.
16 Jun 1991	F-ODVF A310-304	445	Returned 15 August 1991
Boeing 737			
4 Aug 1978	CP-2313 737-2K3	21494	Winglets added by 2001. Named *Ezekiel 36:36*: 'Then the nations that are left all around you shall know that I am the Lord; I have rebuilt the ruined places and replanted that which was desolate. I am the Lord; I have spoken, and I will do it.' See addendum for further details.

Date	Identity	C/N	Fate
20 Dec 1996	CP-2313 Boeing 737-3A1	28389	Named *Paititi*. Transferred to Varig, 2007.
Aug 2000	CP-2391 Boeing 737-382	24366	Named *Tunari*. Transferred to Varig in January 2005. Leased from Pegasus Aviation US.
Boeing 757			
Dec 2004	N756NA Boeing 757-26N	32488	Returned from lease with GECAS, June 2005.
Dec 2004	N958PG Boeing 757-236	24118	Returned from lease with Pegasus Aviation, 29 September 2005.
Boeing 767			
23 Dec 2002	CP-2425 767-3P6ER	23764	Leased. Sustained substantial damage at Santa Cruz during a hard landing 7 August 2004, following a flight from Miami. Returned to Pegasus Aviation 2006. Named *Madrileño* and used for the initial flight to Madrid in November 2004.
29 Nov 1989	G-BLKV 767-204	23072	Short-term charter from Britannia Airways. Returned 31 Jan 1990.
Fokker F 27			
Aug 1985	CP-2013 Fokker F-27-200	10138	Donated by the Netherlands to Bolivia. Originally named *Reina Beatrix*, but later named *Guayaramerín* after a town in Bolivia. To the FAB as EB-91.
Nov 1987	CP-2165 Fokker F-27 600	10592	Damaged beyond repair on 22 December 1994 during take-off from Guayaramerín, following the number 2 engine going into auto-feather mode. As a result, take-off was abandoned and the aircraft overran the runway and crashed into trees 394ft (120m) from the runway.
Jul 1995	CP-2282 Fokker F-27-400M	10600	Originally ex FAB and leased to LAB. Returned to FAB by 2000. This was a military version, fitted with a large cargo door.

Other books you might like:

Airlines Series, Vol. 6

Historic Commercial Aircraft Series, Vol. 3

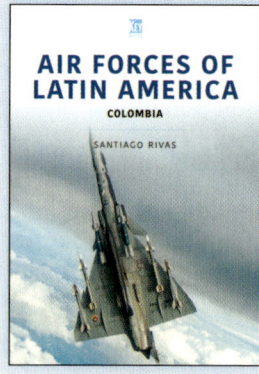
Air Forces Series, Vol. 5

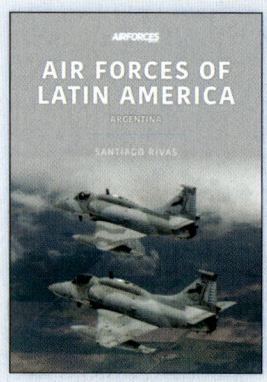
Air Forces Series, Vol. 1

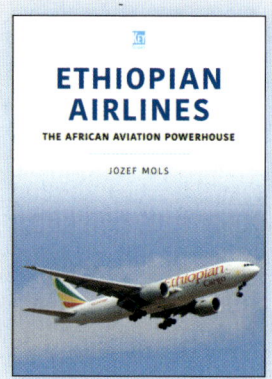
Airlines Series, Vol. 2

Airlines Series, Vol. 4

For our full range of titles please visit:
shop.keypublishing.com/books

VIP Book Club

Sign up today and receive
TWO FREE E-BOOKS

Be the first to find out about our forthcoming book releases and receive exclusive offers.

Register now at **keypublishing.com/vip-book-club**

Our VIP Book Club is a 100% spam-free zone, and we will never share your email with anyone else. You can read our full privacy policy at: privacy.keypublishing.com